# AMERICA
# DREAMING

# AMERICA DREAMING

## HOW YOUTH CHANGED AMERICA IN THE SIXTIES. ★

### LABAN CARRICK HILL

LITTLE, BROWN AND COMPANY
New York ❧ Boston

Also by Laban Carrick Hill: *Harlem Stomp!*

Text copyright © 2007 by Laban Carrick Hill
All rights reserved.

Little, Brown and Company

Hachette Book Group USA
237 Park Avenue, New York, NY 10017
Visit our Web site at www.lb-teens.com

First Edition: November 2007

10 9 8 7 6 5 4 3 2 1

IM

Printed in Singapore

Design by Elise Whittemore-Hill

Hill, Laban Carrick.
    America Dreaming: how youth changed America
in the sixties, by Laban Carrick Hill. — 1st ed.
    p. cm.
Includes bibliographical references and index.
    ISBN-13:987-0-316-00904-1
    ISBN-10: 0-316-00904-0
1.  Social change—United States—History—
20th century—Juvenile literature. 2.  Nineteen
sixties—Juvenile literature.
3.  Baby boom generation—United States—
Juvenile literature.  I. Title.
    HN59.H53 2007
    303.48'4097309046—\dc22                    2006027898

For Elise, always and forever
★ ★ ★ ★ ★ ★ ★ ★ ★ ★ ★

ACKNOWLEDGMENTS

Without Elise Whittemore-Hill and her support, insight, and inspired design, this book would not be what it is today. I would also like to thank Jennifer Hunt for her superb editing, Susan Cohen for her outstanding support and advocacy, Megan Tingley for recognizing I might have something, and Christine Cuccio for her unerring copyediting.

# INTRODUCTION

Whether you call them the "Boomer Generation" or the "Pepsi Generation," those who came of age in the '60s make up the largest and most influential generation ever in American history. Wilder than Gen X, more activist than Gen Y, these youths changed their world like no other generation has before or since. Their music, their language, and their style still define our culture today. *America Dreaming* is more than the story of a youth movement. It's the story of the power and optimism of young people building a world in their own image. Through the lens of pop culture and rock-and-roll, this book tells the story of teens and twenty-somethings who caused a seismic change in American culture.

The full impact of the '60s on American culture has been obscured by the media. When we think of this era, we picture an age of "sex, drugs, and rock-and-roll" radical-

ism. We imagine a period of extremes and excess. This image has been reinforced not only by films—such as the rockumentary *Woodstock*—but also by memoirs celebrating campus protests of the Vietnam War. In truth, only a small minority of '60s teenagers were hippies and/or campus radicals. The real story of the '60s depicts the largest generation in American history coming of age in an unprecedented period of economic growth, and questioning the very basis of our government, culture, and economy. This is the story of young African Americans, young Latinos, young women, young Native Americans, and simply young Americans who woke up one day and decided they wanted something more.

These were teens who dared to dream of an America that was fair and just. *America Dreaming* tells their story.

—LCH

**Romper, bomper, stomper, boo. Tell me, tell me, tell me do. Magic mirror, tell me today. Did all my friends have fun at play? I see Natalie, I see David, I see Ella...**

—"Mirror Song" from *Romper Room*

# *the fifties*
## ROMPER ROOM
### PRESCHOOL FOR THE BOOMER GENERATION

Miss Nancy, the host of the children's television show *Romper Room*, sang this sugary little tune at the end of each episode. She sang it to you if you were part of the Boomer Generation. This generation represented an extraordinary spike in birthrates that began in 1945, at the end of World War II, and continued until 1964. First appearing on air in 1954, *Romper Room* showed

The only massive public project begun in the '50s was the building of the interstate. This put people in their own cars and made it possible for them to drive across the country without using public transportation such as buses, trains, and airplanes.

## BOOMERS BY THE NUMBERS

- 80 million children born between 1946 and 1964
- By 1959, more than 50 million children (30 percent of the population) under the age of 14 lived in the United States.
- There were as many children in 1959 as there were people living in the United States in 1881.
- By 1965, 41 percent of all Americans were under the age of 20. (In 2000, 25.7 percent of the U.S. population was under 18.)

★ ★ ★ ★ ★ ★ ★ ★ ★ ★ ★ ★ ★ ★ ★ ★ ★ ★

**Your future is great in a growing America. Every day 11,000 babies are born in America. This means new business, new jobs, new opportunities.**

—sign in the New York City subway in the 1950s

just how much America had changed from a country at war to one of rebirth. The half-hour show essentially televised a preschool class in which Miss Nancy would read from books to seven or eight kids on the set and teach the alphabet, manners, and values in a *gentle way*. Like this popular show, America was all about raising children. The idealized *Romper Room* world marked the degree to which the country had changed from a society in crisis to a community in renewal—or rather, a community preoccupied with raising children. In short, 1950s America became essentially one giant playpen.

After fifteen years of decline and suffering that began on Black Tuesday, October 29, 1929, with the stock market crash, continuing through the 1930s with the Depression and mass unemployment, and morphing into the horror of World War II, America was ready for prosperity. Winning the war raised America to global supremacy, and the country hungered to taste the fruits of this success. Americans were tired of the social and political demands of the previous decade and a half. They were desperately eager for the American Dream—marriage, children, good jobs, a home. The peace dividend of winning the war made all this possible to a large percentage of the population for the first time in history. America was no longer in a depression, and the economy was no longer pouring every cent into the war effort.

The U.S. government helped the boom along by providing returning soldiers with the Serviceman's Readjustment Act, commonly known as the G.I. bill, which Congress passed in 1944. This program offered veterans unemployment compensation, medical benefits, loans to start new businesses and buy a home, and tuition benefits for higher education. The result was that the government infused the economy with hundreds of millions of dollars just when it was needed most. This spurred an economic boom, which led to the largest expansion in American his-

# Every **seven seconds**, a woman became **pregnant.** This added about a city the size of **Los Angeles** to the U.S. population each year.

—historian William Manchester

tory. With the U.S. government directing public funds into private spaces and private goods, not public services—such as dams, rural electrification, executing the war, and other large government projects—as was done in the previous decades, there was a profound change in the American psyche. The result was that all segments of society were improving their positions. This improvement was not in relation to one another, but in relation to every person's past and that of his or her family. This meant that everyone in the country was doing at least a little better than they had before. In the beginning, that was enough to fuel a kind of euphoria not seen previously in America. For the first time it appeared possible that the country would achieve that ideal of the "city on a hill" that was first imagined by the early Puritans. This new economic security fueled a confidence in the future and a dream that America could truly become the first utopian society.

## BUILD IT AND THEY WILL COME

The first step to achieving the good life was to own a home. A home represented the embodiment of the American Dream. Home ownership offered all the possibilities that Hollywood films and television sitcoms depicted: the perfect family where dad had a good job, mom was the doting housewife, the kids went to good schools and, eventually, college. America was meant to be just like the television shows *Leave It to Beaver*, *Father Knows Best*, and a dozen others. In these sitcoms the dad went off each day to work, the mom stayed home and took care of the kids, who somehow got into some domestic trouble that was resolved by the end of the half hour.

Two brothers, Alfred and William J. Levitt, recognized this shift in the culture. The skills they learned building military housing and instant airfields in the

### SPOCK BABIES

Pediatrician Benjamin Spock, MD, wrote the child-rearing bible for Boomer parents, *The Common Sense Book of Baby and Child Care* (1946). This book changed the way Americans raised their children. His most common advice was: **"Trust yourself, you know more than you think you do."** This was a revolutionary idea when traditional baby manuals offered authoritarian directives on strict feeding schedules and rigid routines. Instead, Spock mirrored the optimism of the era by reinforcing that parents were their own experts. They had the power to raise a perfect child without interference by so-called authorities. Spock was one of the first influential proponents of what would become a search for self-fulfillment in the 1960s.

Pacific during the war taught them that the old ways of building were obsolete, simply because those methods took too long. Together the brothers broke down the construction of a house into twenty-seven separate steps and trained twenty-seven separate crews to specialize in just one step. Borrowing Henry Ford's mass production system for cars, William Levitt flipped the model. Instead of moving a car along an assembly line past each workstation, the workers themselves would move from one house to the next. Each house stood on a 60-by-100-foot plot, and the crews would perform their individualized tasks and move on. One crew would pour the foundation. The next would build the frame. This would continue until all twenty-seven construction crews had completed their tasks and a new house was finished.

The Levitts revolutionized the way homes were built. In the past, the typical builder constructed fewer than five houses a year. By 1948, the Levitts were able to build 180 houses a week, which broke down to thirty-six houses a day. "Eighteen houses completed on the shift from eight to noon, and eighteen more houses finished on the shift from twelve-thirty to four-thirty," noted Bill Levitt. Because of these innovations, it was possible for ordinary people—people who had never thought of themselves as middle-class before—to own an inexpensive, attractive home. The first housing development built by the Levitts was located twenty miles outside New York City on Long Island. It contained 17,000 homes, and 82,000 people lived there. Schools, churches, and grocery and other retail stores quickly followed.

This plan for building homes was soon duplicated all over the country. In a matter of years, suburban communities just outside cities sprouted where farms used to be, and families achieved the American Dream. Along with a new home, people had good jobs that paid a decent wage, and they could afford things that just a few years before were beyond reach: new cars, televisions, washing machines, refrigerators, and a host of other appliances and technolo-

gies that made life easier and more convenient. Suddenly, it seemed that everyone was affluent, not just the rich.

Economist John Maynard Keynes coined the term "relentless consumption" to describe the new era, meaning that as long as industry produced enough goods and services to employ most of the country, people would have the financial means to purchase these goods and services and better their lives. The argument concluded that nearly *all* economic and social issues would be solved because goods and services would be plentiful and affordable, and

*The Levittowner*

**PRICE: $10,990        $67 A MONTH**

people would have the income to purchase them.

On the surface, this seemed to work exceedingly well. Not only were plenty of homes being built, but other businesses were popping up to fill needs that hadn't existed before. With everyone so busy enjoying improved lives, families didn't always have time to make dinner. McDonald's filled the void and changed the way a family ate together. With more dollars in their pockets, families could afford to travel and see the country. Holiday Inns sprung up along the new interstates, with affordable accommodations. This affluence also gave people more choices in how they spent their money. To give consumers this variety of choices in one convenient location, shopping malls spread across America where dozens of stores

This is Levittown! All yours for $58. You're a lucky fellow, Mr. Veteran. Uncle Sam and the world's largest builder have made it possible for you to live in a charming house in a delightful community without having to pay for them with your eyeteeth.

—an advertisement for the Levitt brothers' homes

An aerial photograph of Levittown, PA.

*Get It New!*

New is good, better, best.

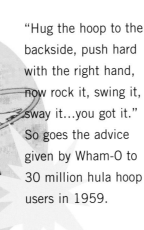

"Hug the hoop to the backside, push hard with the right hand, now rock it, swing it, sway it...you got it." So goes the advice given by Wham-O to 30 million hula hoop users in 1959.

Advertisers discovered in the '50s that the best way to get consumers to identify with their product was to humanize it. Alka Seltzer's Speedy was one of the most successful of these campaigns.

competed to give shoppers a cornucopia of products. All of these goods and services changed the way America lived, and at the time it all seemed for the better. Life was indeed very good and quickly getting better.

One person's paradise, however, can be another's hell. Social critic Lewis Mumford tartly characterized these suburban utopias as actual suburban dystopias:

> A multitude of uniform, unidentifiable houses, lined up inflexibly, at uniform distances on uniform roads, in a treeless command of waste, inhabited by people of the same class, the same incomes, the same age group, witnessing the same television performances, eating the same tasteless prefabricated foods, from the same freezers, conforming in every outward and inward respect to a common mold manufactured in the same central metropolis. Thus the ultimate effect of the suburban escape in our time is, ironically, a low-grade uniform environment from which escape is impossible.

For Mumford and many others, the new suburban communities were a wasteland, soulless and culturally empty. These critics had a point. Everything was new, and if it was new, it was not broken, dirty, or worn out, like just about everything had been during the Depression and World War II.

Never has so much been available to so many of us as now...that *open sesame* to wealth and freedom... freedom from tedium, space, work and your own inexperience.

—Food writer Poppy Cannon in *Life* magazine, 1954

6

Writer John Updike wrote the satiric poem "Superman" in 1954 to poke fun at the era's unfounded optimism:

> I drive my car to supermarket,
> . . .
> A superlot is where I park it,
> And Super Suds are what I buy.

Many saw the social conformity of the era as not just soulless but dangerous to the culture as a whole. Columbia University sociologist and philosopher C. Wright Mills wrote two groundbreaking volumes on the subject: *White Collar* (1951) and *The Power Elite* (1956). In these criticisms of contemporary culture, Mills warned that America was becoming an affluent society without purpose. He argued against materialism and the predictability of corporate life. Around the same time, social scientist David Riesman examined how the increasing power of corporate and government organizations influenced national character. The result of Riesman's study was the critique *The Lonely Crowd* (1950), in which he suggests that every age produces certain personality types: Wars create warriors, and an era of expansion creates adventurers. He concluded that the '50s required people who were flexible and willing to accommodate others to win approval: in short, people pleasers. This was the era of conformity. According to Riesman's estimation, these types of people were essential to big organizations, but they were not innovators or visionaries.

Economist John Kenneth Galbraith attacked what he saw as a fatal flaw in the era. In his bestseller *The Affluent Society* he challenged Keynes's economic theories about the primacy of affluence. Galbraith argued that what Keynes's notion of investing in production and acquisition really accomplished was an impoverished society, starved of public services. He wrote that in placing so much faith in the general curative powers of increased production, America was inviting grave social ills. In order for a community to function well, "even the stalwart conservative who dares not to venture out in the street at night, pays heavily for private security guards, thinks often about kidnapping and hesitates on occasion to drink the water or breathe the air, must, on occasion, wonder if keeping public services at a minimum is really a practical formula for expanding his personal liberty."

The questions these critics raised would not have an immediate effect on America, but these dissentions sowed the seeds of discontent that set the stage for the coming '60s decade.

Interestingly, horror movies as well as comics became incredibly popular during the '50s. When **The Invasion of the Body Snatchers** hit the screens in 1956, screenwriter Ron Rosenbaum explained that the film was "about the horror of being in the 'burbs, about neighbors whose lives had so lost their individual distinctiveness they could be taken over by alien vegetable pods—*and no one would know the difference.*"

## PARANOIA REIGNS SUPREME

The entire country seemed to be suffering from post-traumatic stress disorder. Every time a threat appeared on the horizon, America responded dramatically, extensively, and often out of proportion to the actual danger. Suburban homeowners built bomb shelters in their backyards to protect them from the remote possibility that the Soviet Union would drop an atomic bomb in their neighborhood. Local schools held atomic bomb drills in which students hid under their desks, even though a desk or a wall would provide no protection in the event of a real A-bomb explosion.

A family climbing into their backyard bomb shelter.

## PROTECTING UTOPIA

For a country willing to drop an atomic bomb to end a war, it was not surprising that this same country would go to almost any length to protect the greatest economic boom in its history. After fifteen hard years, America wasn't about to let this prosperity disappear. When the USSR, America's ally in the war, became its major political opponent, the country did not stand still. Its mission became to reconstruct the war-torn world and protect it against another totalitarian regime—the USSR, or the Soviet Union.

Throughout its history the Soviet Union had publicly declared itself to be dedicated to world revolution and the overthrow of Western capitalism, in short, America's new suburban and consumer paradise. To that end, the Soviet Union had begun a campaign of encroachment on Europe, where it set up satellite countries, or "People's Democracies," that operated under its control. These countries included most of Eastern Europe (Poland, Czechoslovakia, Hungary, Bulgaria, Rumania, and East Germany), whose borders became known as the "Iron Curtain." In response, the United States initiated the Marshall Plan to rehabilitate Western Europe after World War II through an infusion of economic support.

Elsewhere in the world, the United States took a military stance to staunch the "red tide" of Communism. In 1949, China had fallen to Communist forces, and the Korean peninsula was divided along the 38th parallel into South Korea and communist North Korea. When communist forces crossed into South Korea, U.S. forces arrived in June 1950 to stop them in what was then called a "police action" and is now called the Korean War. In July 1953, the war ended with an armistice agreement, but a peace treaty was never signed. This stalemate in Asia and Europe eventually evolved into the Cold War—a war without explosions and fire. As long as neither side made encroachments into the other's territory, an uneasy peace would remain and America's political, social, and economic security would be preserved.

On the home front, this meant protecting America against "otherness," or rather, anything that didn't fit within the consumer culture. Already the country had reduced the possibility of difference with the restrictive immigration policies that went back to the 1920s. For approximately thirty years almost no one was allowed to immigrate to the States, except a trickle from Europe. This created a country that was predominantly white and of European background. As a result the only easily identifiable outsiders were African Americans. The color of their skin made them an easy mark for exclusion. This was achieved throughout the country with the Jim Crow laws. "Jim Crow" was slang for the racist rules and laws that separated blacks and whites. Because of this, many of these new suburbs barred black families. Levittown, the country's emblematic new community, did not allow an African-American family into the development until

# WHITES ONLY

1957, ten years after the first house was built, and this could occur only with around-the-clock police protection for the black family. In addition to housing, blacks were barred from many public spaces and jobs.

> **The *World Book* annual list of new words and phrases for 1954 included the word "desegregate."**

Politicians were quick to exploit this fear of "otherness" or anything that was different. Perhaps the most despicable misuse of the public's trust was exemplified by Senator Joseph R. McCarthy, who conducted hearings before the Senate Committee on Government Operations.

In 1950, McCarthy, a Wisconsin Republican, used the country's general anxiety about a Communist threat to make numerous charges—usually with little evidence—that certain public officials and other individuals were Communists or cooperated with the Communists. In these hearings McCarthy berated and threatened witnesses and labeled them Communists publicly. Eventually, the Senate censured him for his behavior. But before McCarthy's downfall, many of the individuals who were accused but never convicted were blacklisted from their professions, particularly Hollywood writers, directors, and actors. This meant that they could no longer get and hold jobs in their fields. Being branded a Communist or a Communist sympathizer ruined many lives long after McCarthyism disappeared. The blacklists remained well into the '60s and kept people from being able to make a living.

This general fear and anxiety in the country created a culture of intolerance that was clearly vulnerable to and deserving of backlash.

Senator
Joseph R. McCarthy

## WHADDAYA GOT? BOREDOM AND CONTEMPT

Although there was real danger to the expansion of American ideals in the rest of the world, the country itself was relatively safe and content. One unexpected threat to this new paradise—this American Dream—came from within. The children growing up in all those tranquil cul-de-sacs were bored.

Perfection was boring. An endless future of idyllic days spent in communities with perfectly manicured lawns, lovely homes, well-behaved pets, and ideal families could be horribly dull and predictable. Everyone wants a little excitement—the unexpected—in his or her life. This was particularly true for a generation who never experienced the hardship and unpredictability of the Depression and World War II—namely the kids.

This restlessness manifested itself almost immediately in the films, comic books, and other media of the era. The theme of the juvenile delinquent loose in the community became a popular plot in films. One of the first and most popular of this genre was *The Wild One*, the landmark film of '50s rebellion. Premiering under the title *Hot Blood*, it was the first feature to examine outlaw motorcycle gang violence in America.

By today's standards, *The Wild One* was definitely tame, but what resonated in the film was one particular scene. The young, attractive waitress in the town's café/bar was disgusted by the boorishness of the gang's leader, played by Marlon Brando, and asked impatiently, "What are you rebelling against?" A side-burned, leather-clad Brando famously replied, "Whaddaya got?"

Brando's belligerent pose resonated with young people and inspired a slew of juvenile delinquent movies. This culminated two years later in *Rebel Without a Cause* (1955), a movie starring the legendary James Dean, who portrayed a confused teen questioning his parents' authority. *Rebel Without a Cause* offered for the first time a sympathetic perspective on the misunderstood American youth. The film became an instant classic, in part because it looked at the world of the conformist mid-'50s from the point of view of the restless, misunderstood middle-class youth, but also because James Dean died in a car accident one month before the release of the film. By dying so young, Dean became an instant legend—the mythic, eternal rebel whose promise would never be fulfilled, and who would never suffer the indignity of growing old.

While some found the American Dream simply dull and constricting, others were troubled by what else they saw in suburbia: monotony, soullessness, cultural emptiness, and materialism. For these people, life was not like an episode of *Leave It to Beaver*, the popular TV show about a traditional, suburban family. Their lives did not mirror a world where the day's big crisis was "the Beave" forgetting to do his homework. Ironically, as much as the majority of Americans wanted to buy into this fantasy of conformity, nobody's life was really all that perfect.

**HOT BLOOD**

"Hot feelings hit terrifying heights in this story that really boils over!"

The criticism of this new life exhibited itself in a variety of ways. For teens, comic books became one of the major outlets for rebellion. Clearly not literature meant to improve moral character, the most popular comics exploited teens' desires to escape their humdrum suburban life. Some of the most popular were horror comics—gruesome tales of the undead and vampires—that touched a deep psychic desire in teens for excitement. Quickly, adults decided that comic books were corrupting the younger generation. Adults responded to this new threat to utopia much like they did to communism. Like McCarthy's interrogation committee, the Comic Magazine Association of America was formed in May of 1954. This new association created a "code" that banned popular horror comics.

Luckily, this new turn did not deter William Gaines, horror comics' most creative voice. Instead, Gaines cast his inspired gaze toward satirizing the society that was set on shutting him down. He gave his editors the green light to start a new kind of humor magazine. It was titled *Mad* and was completely unique because it skewered conformist '50s culture. Each issue offered up a satirical, skeptical portrayal of American life, which clearly was taking itself too seriously. *Mad* ridiculed everything and everyone. Without a doubt, adolescents recognized the magazine as the perfect antidote to the pompous and pretentious adult world. Ironically, *Mad* did for youth culture what horror comics never would have done: It put a name to their discontent.

The writer who did more to expose the hypocrisy in contemporary culture, however, was J.D. Salinger. His novel *The Catcher in the Rye* caused such a stir when it was published in 1951 that it was banned in many communities. Still, it became a bestseller because it spoke directly to the emotions of teen and adult readers alike. The main character, Holden Caulfield, sees adulthood as full of superficiality and hypocrisy, or in his word "phoniness,"

# THE Catcher IN THE Rye

In this excerpt from *The Catcher in the Rye*, Holden Caulfield describes his old boarding school and phonies:

One of the biggest reasons I left Elkton Hills was because I was surrounded by phonies. That's all. They were coming in the goddam window. For instance, they had this hea[d]ter, Mr. Haas, that was the phoniest b[astard I] ever met in my life. Ten times wor[se than] Thurmer. On Sundays, for ins[tance, he] went around shaking han[ds with all the] parents when they d[rove up. He'd] be charming as [hell and all. Except if some] boy had litt[le] You sh[ould] my r[oom] boy'[s] loo[k] father was one [with very big sh[oulders and big old corny] shoes, then old [Haas would go up to] them and give t[hem] talk, for maybe[half an hour. Then he'd go] parents. I ca[n't stand that] stuff. It [drives me crazy. It] makes m[e so depressed] I go cra[zy. I hated that god-] dam Elk[ton Hills.]

A well I bless
my soul
What's wrong
with me?
I'm itching like
a man on a
fuzzy tree
My friends say
I'm actin' wild
as a bug
I'm in love
I'm all shook up
Mm mm oh, oh,
yeah, yeah!

—lyrics from Elvis Presley hit "All Shook Up"

12

AMERICA DREAMING

and childhood as the true sanctuary of honesty, curiosity, innocence, and purity. Holden symbolizes pure, unfettered individuality in the face of cultural oppression.

## ALL SHOOK UP

While many white youths might have been rebelling for the sake of rebelling, others were looking beyond the manicured boundaries of their neat little communities for a more interesting world. One of the first places these white suburban youths looked was in black culture. Because African Americans were excluded from much of America's rising mass culture, the white youths were drawn to this forbidden and exotic-seeming community. Perhaps the best avenues for exploring black culture were the radio stations that played a new kind of music called rhythm and blues. R&B was a high-energy mix of several traditional black musical styles: field, church, and juke joint.

One white teenager was particularly inspired by the music he heard on these black stations. His actions, according to *Rolling Stone* magazine, began one of the most influential and lasting musical traditions in America: rock-and-roll. Rock-and-roll was born on July 5, 1954, when a nineteen-year-old truck driver for Crown Electric entered the Memphis Recording Studio owned by Sam Phillips. This was the moment when Elvis Presley opened his mouth and sang "That's All Right (Mama)," a cover of a 1947 tune written and first sung by black singer-guitarist Arthur Crudup. Elvis fused the several musical styles of R&B into a high-energy, expressive sound. Backup guitarist Scotty Moore remembered in 1991 about the session: "We just sort of shook our heads and said, 'Well, that's fine, but good God, they'll run us out of town.'" Tolerance for anything other than mainstream culture was in short supply.

Though the record did not sell very well, it was the first note in a great tidal wave of new sound. Over the next few years some of the greatest rock-and-roll classics were cut:

## "Elvis Presley is the greatest cultural force in the twentieth century."

—Leonard Bernstein
Classical composer and conductor

## "This hooby-dooby, oop-shoop, ootie-ootie, boom-boom, de-addy boom, scoobledy goobledy clump— is trash."

—The *Denver Post* commenting on rock-and-roll

"An unrelenting, socking syncopation that sounds like a bull whip; a choleric saxophone honking mating call sounds; an electric guitar turned up so loud that its sound shatters and splits; a vocal group that shudders and exercises violently to the beat while roughly chanting either a near-nonsense phrase or a moronic lyric in hillbilly idiom..."

—*Time*, June 18, 1956, in an article describing rock-and-roll

RECORD COMPANY

Hi Lo Music BMI

Vocal U-156

MYSTERY TRAIN
(Parker-Phillips)
ELVIS PRE

# HIPSTER LINGO

| | |
|---|---|
| **Axe** | a musical instrument |
| **Baby** | a loved one |
| **Bad** | good |
| **Bag** | someone's particular interest or talent |
| **Beat** | tired or exhausted |
| **Blow your top** | to get overly upset or angry |
| **Bomb, The** | someone or something extremely cool |
| **Bread** | money |
| **Bring down, Bringdown** | to depress; someone who's depressed |
| **Bug** | annoy |
| **Cat** | a cool person |
| **Chick** | a young, pretty girl |
| **Crazy** | weird |
| **Crumb** | someone who is disrespectful |
| **Dad, Daddy-o** | what hipsters call other guys |
| **Dig** | totally understand |
| **Disk jockey, Deejay, DJ** | someone who announces and selects records on the radio |
| **Down by law** | someone who has paid their dues |
| **Drag** | someone or something that depresses |
| **End, The** | crazy, incredible |

- The ultimate party song of all time, "Louie, Louie" by the Kingsmen
- The historic thirty-sixth take of "Maybellene" that turned Chuck Berry into a household name
- The rockabilly sound of Memphis Recording Studio powerhouses Jerry Lee Lewis and Johnny Cash
- The crazy frenzy of Little Richard's "Tutti Frutti"

Rock-and-roll was here to stay. This music brought to life the same kind of rebellious attitude and energy that movies like *The Wild One* and *Rebel Without a Cause* were able to tap into. The difference, though, was that it didn't simply celebrate nihilism and powerlessness. Instead, it opened the picket fences of the dominant white culture to a truly entertaining—and truly American—musical tradition.

## THE MARKETING OF ROCK-AND-ROLL

The rise in popularity of rock-and-roll did not happen through traditional avenues. Rock groups were first recorded by independent record producers. At the beginning of the '50s, the recording equipment to produce records cost approximately one thousand dollars. Anyone could open a recording studio in their basement, and many did. Sam Phillips's Sun Records was a tiny recording studio in Memphis that got most of its business from walk-ins who wanted to record something and paid to cut a record. Elvis had originally entered the studio to make a record of gospel songs for his mother, but Phillips recognized the young nineteen-year-old as something special. Phillips also recorded such rock pioneers as Jerry Lee Lewis, Carl Perkins, and Johnny Cash.

While production was inexpensive, distribution became equally simple. The jukebox industry at the time was run by the mafia. Because the mob was interested only in profits, not the morality of young people, mobsters were happy to stock their jukeboxes with whatever recordings kids wanted to hear at the local drive-in, bowling alley, or drugstore. At the same time, young DJs like

Alan Freed in Cincinnati spun rock-and-roll platters on their radio shows despite disapproval from the older generation. Both the mob and disk jockeys let the marketplace determine what product was available, and in doing so they were a step ahead of the large media companies. That would change, of course, when RCA bought Elvis's contract and master recordings from Sun Records in 1957 for a measly $35,000. Other major labels would follow. The phenomenon of rock-and-roll showed not only just how powerful the youth marketplace was, but also that not everything was mass-market driven.

## GO, CAT, GO!

The Beats took it even further. Beats were counterculture mavens who railed against conformity by celebrating the underside of America, the hidden America. That meant not only black culture but also street culture, drug culture, and whatever else was decidedly not the American Dream. The Beats venerated whatever was taboo, and in a conservative society like America in the '50s, there were many taboos. A 1954 article in the *New York Times Magazine* titled "This Is the Beat Generation" by Clellon Holmes quoted writer Jack Kerouac as saying, "You know, this is really a beat generation." Holmes went on to explain what that meant:

> The origins of the word "beat" are obscure, but the meaning is only too clear to most Americans. More than mere weariness, it implies the feeling of having been used, of being raw. It involves a sort of nakedness of mind, and, ultimately, of soul, a feeling of being reduced to a bedrock of consciousness. In short, it means being undramatically pushed up against the wall of oneself. A man is beat whenever he goes for broke and wagers the sum of his resources on a single number; and the young generation has done that continually from their youth.

| | |
|---|---|
| **Flip** | go crazy; an eccentric person |
| **Flip your lid** | blow your top |
| **Gas** | stir up feelings, something that moves you |
| **Gig** | a paying job |
| **Gone** | crazy |
| **Hand me that/ some skin** | shake my hand; give me five |
| **Hep, hip** | used to describe someone who understands well |
| **Hipster** | someone who follows the different types of bop jazz |
| **Jake** | okay |
| **Junk** | heroin |
| **Kill** | excite |
| **Out of this world** | incredible |
| **Out to lunch** | lame |
| **Pad** | bed, home, apartment |
| **Scene** | a place, atmosphere, environment |
| **Send** | move emotionally |
| **Snap your cap** | flip your lid |
| **Solid** | dependable, cool |
| **Square** | unknowing |
| **Wild** | crazy |
| **Witch doctor** | a minister or priest |

"When I am in my painting, I'm not aware of what I'm doing. It's only after a sort of 'get acquainted' period that I see what I have been about. I have no fears about making changes, destroying the image, etc., because the painting has a life of its own."

—Jackson Pollock, *Possibilities I, Winter* 1947–48

## WHAT'S IT A PICTURE OF?

During the '50s, visual artists rebelled against conformity by questioning the very assumptions of what a painting represents. This new movement was called abstract expressionism. Rather than a painting being merely a picture of the concrete world—however distorted or interpreted—painters began to explore the basic elements of painting as ends in themselves. These works of art expressed the painters' vision purely through the use of form and color. Now considered to be the first American artistic movement of worldwide importance, the abstract expressionists can be divided into two groups: action painting (typified by artists such as Jackson Pollock, Willem de Kooning, Franz Kline, and Philip Guston), which put the focus on the physical action involved in painting, and color field painting (practiced by Mark Rothko and Kenneth Noland, among others), which was primarily concerned with exploring the effects of pure color on a canvas.

Clearly, the "beat" attitude did not promote the kind of optimism and abundance that the dominant culture reveled in. Kerouac was able to capture this "beat" sensibility, its aspirations and soul, in his explosive novel *On the Road*. The novel wore the clothes of fiction but was really a nonfiction account of Kerouac's own experiences. In direct opposition to the "company man" mentality, *On the Road* celebrated the individual in all his eccentricities and shortcomings. Unlike the careful, methodical, hardworking, and conscientious approach the '50s morality promoted, Kerouac wrote the novel in a blinding, nonstop, adrenaline- and speed-inspired burst of creativity. Essentially, the manuscript was one long paragraph typed on a continuous roll of paper, which his publisher broke down into paragraphs and sections. The novel portrayed an underground America full of what critic Ted Morgan has described as "pure, meaningless, abstract motion." The main character, Sal Paradise, follows his hero, Dean Moriarty, ricocheting across the country like a rubber Super Ball™ hurled into space. The main energy of these men is their drive to exist outside the mainstream. They do not want to play by the rules of society. They avoid work whenever possible, and when they have to work, they take meaningless, dead-end jobs. All this was antithetical to the mores of the era. In the novel, Sal describes exactly the kind of life he is searching for:

The only people for me are the mad ones, the ones who are mad to live, mad to talk, mad to be saved, desirous of everything at the same time, the ones who never yawn or say a commonplace thing, but burn, burn, burn like fabulous yellow roman candles exploding like spiders across the stars and in the middle you see the blue centerlight pop and everybody goes "Awww!"

Kerouac wasn't alone in his search for what he called the "beatific." Like Kerouac, poet Allen Ginsberg was part of this group that included writer William Burroughs, Neal Cassidy, poet LeRoi Jones, and a number of other artists, hipsters, and writers on both the East and West coasts. Ginsberg came to prominence with the publication of his first book of poems, *Howl and Other Poems*. It was originally published by City Lights Books in the fall of 1956. Subsequently seized by U.S. customs and San Francisco police, the book was the subject of a long court trial at which a series of poets and professors persuaded the court that the book was not obscene. In the title poem,

"Howl," Ginsberg sets out to celebrate all that is not suburban conformity. He begins by paying homage to all nonconformists: "I saw the best minds of my generation destroyed by madness, starving hysterical naked..." He also rails against the decadent materialistic society, which he likens to Moloch, who in the Bible was the god of the Canaanites and Phoenicians to whom children were sacrificed.

Ironically, while the greatest boom in America's history was welcomed by most, the few who found fault in this prosperity would come to define the next era— the '60s.

**Moloch whose love is endless oil and stone! Moloch whose soul is electricity and banks! Moloch whose poverty is the specter of genius! Moloch whose fate is a cloud of sexless hydrogen!**

—from "Howl," by Allen Ginsberg

The Beat Generation: (l to r) Hal Chase, Jack Kerouac, Allen Ginsberg, and William S. Burroughs.

# I WANNA HOLD YOUR HAND

When a hatless, coatless John F. Kennedy stepped up to the podium in wintry Washington, D.C., to deliver his inaugural presidential address, he did nothing less than recast the national image. At forty-three, Kennedy was not only the youngest president in this country's history, he was also the first president to be born in the twentieth century.

Kennedy took the presidential oath just when the country needed him. America was experiencing an identity crisis. For the previous fifteen years, the country had lived through the greatest economic expansion in the world's history. The United States had moved from a backward, third-rate power before World War II to the most powerful nation in the free world. The only country that challenged its supremacy was the Communist Soviet Union. What this unprecedented transformation meant to the nation's citizens was still not clear. So much seemed possible.

"Ask not what your country can do for you; ask what you can do for your country."

—President John F. Kennedy, Inaugural Address, January 20, 1961

"But what now shall Americans *do* with the greatness of their nation? **And is it great enough?** And is it great in the right way?"

★ ★ ★ ★ ★ ★ ★ ★ ★ ★ ★ ★ ★ ★ ★ ★ ★ ★ ★ ★ ★ ★ ★ ★ ★ ★ ★ ★ ★ ★ ★ ★ ★ ★ ★ ★

Several years earlier, President Eisenhower set up the President's Commission on National Goals. Around the same time, Nelson Rockefeller, one of the heirs to John D. Rockefeller's oil empire, funded a special studies project through one of his foundations. Both of the reports from these studies became bestsellers, but nothing really resulted from them. In 1960, *Life* magazine featured a series of articles on the theme of "national purpose." Asking questions like, "But what now shall Americans *do* with the greatness of their nation? And is it great enough?

And is it great in the right way?" Poet and critic Archibald MacLeish wrote, "But it isn't the Russians, now, it's ourselves....We feel that we've lost our way in the woods, that we don't know where we are going—if anywhere." These efforts all identified a crisis in the American sense of purpose, but none of them really provided an answer. They simply raised more questions.

Over the previous decade it seemed everything had changed and the country had not figured out what to make of it. Since the nineteenth century, the morals of the country had been based on such character traits as self-discipline, delayed gratification, and restraint. These values were essential to progress and economic expansion. If workers were lazy and undisciplined, nothing would get built. In conflict with these values was the reality of the marketplace. All these goods and services so conscientiously manufactured would not be purchased if consumers did not buy into an opposing set of values: instant gratification and unrestrained pleasure. In short, self-denial conflicted directly with the needs of an expanding economy. In order for the economy to continue to grow, consumers needed to be unrestrained and to exceed the borders of responsible consumption.

Kennedy was able to harness the incredibly expansive idea of national possibility and offered an answer to the seeming contradiction between the values that led to prosperity and the values that were essential to its survival. In his acceptance speech at the Democratic convention in the summer of 1960, Kennedy called this new era the "New Frontier":

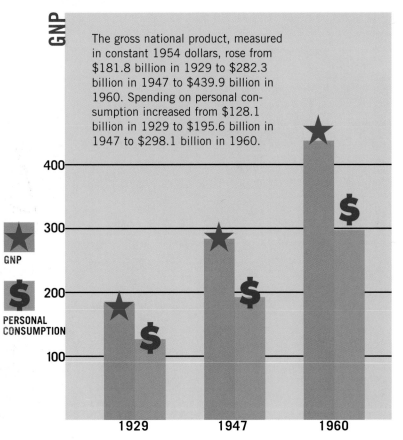

GNP

The gross national product, measured in constant 1954 dollars, rose from $181.8 billion in 1929 to $282.3 billion in 1947 to $439.9 billion in 1960. Spending on personal consumption increased from $128.1 billion in 1929 to $195.6 billion in 1947 to $298.1 billion in 1960.

GNP

$ PERSONAL CONSUMPTION

400

300

200

100

1929    1947    1960

> We stand today on the edge of a New Frontier—the frontier of the 1960s—a frontier of unknown opportunities and perils—a frontier of unfulfilled hopes and threats.... The New Frontier of which I speak is not a set of promises—it is a set of challenges. It sums up not what I intend to offer the American people, but what I intend to ask them. It appeals to their pride, not their pocketbook—it holds out the promise of more sacrifice instead of more security.

With these words Kennedy was able to marry American prosperity to a mission: unfettered consumption was not only good for America but also for the world. He challenged America to do nothing less than redefine its values: Hedonism was good because it drove prosperity, but our good fortune could also improve the world. Kennedy was saying that now that we have achieved this incredible prosperity, we must use it for the good of everyone, not for selfish personal pleasures. It was our duty to take our good fortune and use it to better the world. To quote a phrase often repeated at the time: "A rising tide would lift all boats."

## CARROT AND STICK DIPLOMACY ★ ★ ★ ★ ★ ★ ★ ★ ★ ★ ★ ★ ★ ★ ★ ★ ★ ★ ★ ★ ★ ★ ★ ★ ★ ★ ★ ★

Two lasting legacies of Kennedy's presidency were the establishment of the Peace Corps and the Army Special Forces. Both programs worked toward the same goal: promoting democracy and capitalism around the world. They each approached this goal from opposite ends. The Peace Corps was one of Kennedy's first programs. In his inaugural address he announced, "To those people in the huts and villages of half the globe struggling to break the bonds of mass misery, we pledge our efforts to help them help themselves." In the Peace Corps, volunteers were sent to the poorest regions in the world to make practical differences in those people's lives by trying to improve the catastrophic inadequacies in health care, infrastructure, and economic inequality, among other things. Ironically, the people perhaps most changed by the program were the American volunteers.

"Probably the most significant Peace Corps accomplishment was the education of Americans," suggests historian Irving Bernstein. "They came to understand the people and cultures of the Third World." For the first time, young people were stepping beyond a closed and safe America with extremely restrictive immigration laws to see what the world was really like.

Kennedy called on another elite group of young Americans, this time in the military, to organize the Green Berets, a new section of the Army Special Forces. Unlike the Peace Corps, its mission was not essentially humanitarian. Instead, the Green Berets were formed in response to the long-term instability in the Third World and the Soviet incursions into these vulnerable nations. The Green Berets were designed as a small and elite counterinsurgency force capable of confronting Third World guerrillas. This force was formed in direct response to the success of Fidel Castro and his guerrillas in Cuba two years earlier. They were also organized with other insurgencies around the world in mind, particularly those operating in Vietnam. The Green Berets would not only fight these insurgents, but also train and lead native soldiers against these rebels.

President Kennedy meeting with National Security Committee

## BAY OF PIGS FIASCO

Often, high ideals clash with the real world. For Kennedy, this happened the moment he stepped into the White House. In his first intelligence briefing, Kennedy was informed by CIA Director Allen Dulles about a covert operation to invade Cuba with Cuban exiles trained and armed by the United States. Dulles apparently had assured the president that the invading force would be welcomed by the Cubans and no U.S. military assistance would be needed. The president had to decide immediately whether to go ahead with the invasion.

On New Year's Day in 1959, two years earlier, Fidel Castro and a small army of revolutionaries overthrew the corrupt president of Cuba. President Batista had brutally ruled the country for more than twenty-five years, acting as a tool for American business as well as for the mafia. Batista and his cronies stole millions from the Cuban government and let the great majority of Cubans live in extreme poverty. Castro intended to end the corruption and bring a better life to all Cubans. "The revolution begins now.... It will not be like 1898," Castro announced, "when North Americans came and made themselves masters of our country.... For the first time, the Republic will really be entirely free and the people will have what they deserve."

In Florida and Guatemala, thousands of Cuban exiles were waiting to return to their homeland by force. To stop the invasion, begun under the previous president's administration, would have been nearly impossible. "If we decided to call the whole thing off, I don't know if we could go down there and take the guns away from them," Kennedy observed at the time. Another factor was that Kennedy had criticized the Eisenhower administration for letting Cuba go "red," or Communist. This liberal president saw the people's uprising in Cuba as a sign of the Soviet mentality gaining a foothold in the Western hemisphere. In this atmosphere, Kennedy decided to trust his CIA advisers and go ahead with the invasion. In what would become a pattern that would undermine the government's credibility by the end of the decade, Kennedy was unwilling to acknowledge that his motives were not completely driven by idealism. Powerful American corporations had a large stake in Cuba. If Castro succeeded, these businesses would lose all of their investments, and Kennedy would lose a close neighbor to communism.

In April of 1961, when the invasion began at the Bay of Pigs, it quickly became clear that it would not succeed without air support from the U.S. military. Kennedy was unwilling to allow overt action because he had only signed onto a covert operation by the CIA. On the beaches of the Bay of Pigs, the well-armed Cuban forces were ready for the exiles. In a matter of minutes they cut down the 1,400 men of the exiled Brigade 2506. The Bay of Pigs invasion failed, and the U.S. involvement in it was exposed. Despite this failure, Kennedy and the succeeding administrations throughout the decade did not learn from the experience. Instead, they hardened their commitment to confront communism wherever and whenever it surfaced. In a sense, they resolved never to be humiliated like that again.

Over the next few years, Kennedy and his administration reacted forcefully and decisively against Soviet aggression around the world. At first, this appeared to be a successful strategy, but in the end it would doom American foreign policy.

On August 31, 1961, the Soviets closed the border between East and West Berlin. They erected the concrete and barbed-wire Berlin Wall that ran for 110 miles across Germany. Anyone caught trying to cross into West Berlin was shot. In a defining moment of his presidency

twenty-two months later, in 1963, Kennedy spoke before a crowd of thousands of West Berliners, who were essentially held hostage in their own city. He said:

**There are some who say Communism is the wave of the future. Let them come to Berlin. And there are some who say in Europe and elsewhere, "We can work with the Communists." Let them come to Berlin. And there are even a few who say that it is true that Communism is evil but it permits us to make economic progress. Let them come to Berlin.... All free men, wherever they may live, are citizens of Berlin, and therefore as a free man, I take pride in the words "Ich bin ein Berliner. (I am a Berliner.)"**

These words set Kennedy apart from everyone else in his commitment to fight Communism on every continent. They were hard won after the disaster of the Bay of Pigs, and the Cuban Missile Crisis that occurred one year earlier.

In the spring and summer of 1962, the Soviets dramatically increased their military presence in Cuba and began to set up ballistic missile sites pointing at American cities. By the end of October, the United States had set up a blockade of Cuba to stop Soviet ships from bringing in the missiles. The U.S. also began moving troops to Florida in anticipation of a military invasion. The Strategic Air Command went on nuclear alert, moving to DEFCON 2, one level short of launch, for the first time ever. B-52s were loaded with nuclear bombs and put on alert as well. The world was now at risk of a true nuclear war. After several nerve-racking days, the Soviets backed down and agreed to remove the missiles.

From these events, American politicians concluded that the threat of Communism had to be met forcefully and completely in order to be stopped. This lesson, however, would come to haunt them in the years to come, particularly with regard to the Vietnam War. What few seemed to realize at the time was that nothing can be reduced to a simple ideal or solution, let alone something as complicated as war. America was poised to discover this, painfully and violently, in the coming decade. But in the early years of the '60s, the amazing miracle of American prosperity made happy endings still seem possible.

## THE FINAL FRONTIER

Kennedy did not limit his vision of the United States' influence to just the boundaries of Earth. In 1961, he committed the nation to "landing a man on the moon and returning him safely to the earth."

This proclamation did not come out of the blue. Four years earlier in 1957, the Soviet Union had sent the first satellite, *Sputnik*, into space. Weighing just 184 pounds and orbiting the earth at the lightning speed of 18,000 miles per hour, this launch represented a dawn of a new era as well as a humiliation for the United States inflicted by its bitter enemy. Though *Sputnik* would transmit rudimentary signals for only a few weeks, the symbolism of the act was not lost on the American public. It was truly a

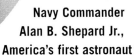

**Navy Commander Alan B. Shepard Jr., America's first astronaut**

shock. America had been experiencing incredible prosperity, which fueled an exaggerated sense of America as standing head and shoulders above the rest of the world. With the Soviet space program, many of these illusions came crashing down. It appeared that American science—and America as a whole—had been left behind, while the Soviet space program triumphed. Nuclear scientist Edward Teller called it a technological Pearl Harbor, referring to Japan's surprise attack on Hawaii that caused the United States to enter World War II.

Critics began declaring that America had lost its edge. We were simply too materialistic and self-indulgent. If only our children had been learning science and mathematics in school, this would never have happened. "The Roman Empire controlled the world because it could build roads," Senate Majority Leader, and future Vice President and President Lyndon B. Johnson proclaimed ominously. "Later, when men moved to sea, the British Empire was dominant because it had ships. Now the Communists have established a foothold in outer space. It is not very reassuring to be told that the next year we will put a 'better' satellite into the air. Perhaps it will even have chrome trim and automatic windshield wipers." Like many others, Johnson believed the very survival of the country was at stake.

In 1961, Kennedy recognized how critical it was to the country's moral stance not simply to be a leader in prosperity but to lead in every area. On May 25 of that year, twenty days after Navy Commander Alan B. Shepard Jr. made a fifteen-minute flight that took him 115 miles above the earth and made him the first American in space, Kennedy outlined his ambitious $7–9 billion moon project. Kennedy proclaimed that landing on the moon "may hold the key to our future on Earth." Although Shepard had gone only a fraction of the distance logged by Uri Gagarin, the first Soviet in space, and his capsule had a top speed of only a quarter as great as Gagarin's, he did maneuver his craft in space by firing small rockets, an achievement the Soviets had not claimed.

"The Soviets have the *Sputniks*, while the Americans, *Kaputniks*."

—A joke told after the Soviets' satellite launch

## A NATION UNITED THROUGH A MASS MARKET

As Kennedy was trying to unite the country around the notion of a national purpose, the nation was gathering every night in front of the television. By 1960, 80 percent of the country had at least one television in their home. The average American watched six hours of TV daily, bringing an entire nation together each evening in front of the tube. Everyone was watching TV shows like *Gunsmoke*, *The Beverly Hillbillies*, and *The Dick Van Dyke Show*. In a sense, America was transformed from isolated regions with unique customs and accents to a nation where everyone owned the same kinds of homes, appliances, cars, and television sets. The marketplace was national, not regional.

By its simple efficiency and overwhelming presence, the national marketplace began to dominate the country. The world had become so interconnected that local ideas, products, and values had become usurped by national ones. In the '50s, rock-and-roll grew through an underground economy of word-of-mouth, mob-owned jukeboxes, and radical DJs. By the '60s, this music marketplace had been replaced by "hit factories" located almost exclusively in New York city.

Rock-and-roll wasn't the only rebel culture to be brought out of the shadows into the mainstream. One of the most popular TV shows in 1963 was *Hootenanny* on ABC. It melded hipster, Beat culture and the folk music scene, which was based in protest music, to make an incredibly innocuous music show out of these subversive cultures. Each week ABC would set up at a college campus and bring a collection of nonthreatening folk groups, such as the

## WONDER

### WHITE BREAD BECOMES A METAPHOR

Only a decade earlier, a shopper would go to a local market to buy a loaf of bread produced by a baker down the street and produce grown a few miles away. By 1960, people were wheeling large shopping carts into vast warehouses of food, newly dubbed "supermarkets," to buy bread produced, not baked, by large national corporations. The derogatory term "white bread" came out of this phenomenon. It describes anything that seems mass-produced, full of air and of little nutritional value, much like the familiar fluffy white loaves being offered by companies like Wonder Bread. Like the name of that company, it seemed truly a marvelous "wonder" how all this was possible.

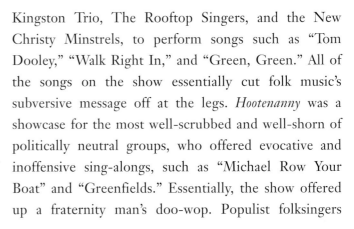

The word **lifestyle** —a word born out of luxury—made its first appearance in *Webster's* dictionary in 1961.

Kingston Trio, The Rooftop Singers, and the New Christy Minstrels, to perform songs such as "Tom Dooley," "Walk Right In," and "Green, Green." All of the songs on the show essentially cut folk music's subversive message off at the legs. *Hootenanny* was a showcase for the most well-scrubbed and well-shorn of politically neutral groups, who offered evocative and inoffensive sing-alongs, such as "Michael Row Your Boat" and "Greenfields." Essentially, the show offered up a fraternity man's doo-wop. Populist folksingers

*Rolling Stone* magazine described how songs were now written, recorded, and made into hits:

INSIDE THE HIT FACTORY

## BRILL BUILDING CHURNS OUT CHART-TOPPING SIXTIES POP

Gerry Goffin finished his day job as a chemist and arrived at his small midtown Manhattan songwriting office around 10 p.m. "Carole had left a melody on a little Norelco tape recorder," he says of his then-wife and songwriting partner, Carole King. "I played it, and the lyrics came to me almost instantly."

The song, "Will You Love Me Tomorrow," was "different from other bullshit we were doing," Goffin says. "It sounded like a standard."

At the same time, Goffin and King toiled for Don Kirshner and Al Nevins, owners of the publishing company Aldon Music and key figures in the "Brill Building sound," which ruled the pop charts in the early Sixties. Located near Times Square at 1619 Broadway in New York, the Brill Building was literally a hit factory: The ten-story office building housed more than 160 music-related businesses—songwriters, publishers, record labels, studios and radio promoters—each trying to outdo the other. You could write a song, sell it to a publisher, cut a demo and sell that to a label just by walking up and down the halls. "It was exciting," says Neil Sedaka, who grew up in the same Brooklyn neighborhood as King and dated her in high school. "We were literally teenagers writing about teenage life."

Goffin and King, along with the other prominent pairings of Sedaka/Howard Greenfield, Barry Mann/Cynthia Weil and Jeff Barry/Ellie Greenwich, actually worked at Aldon, across the street at 1650 Broadway. Each pairing was housed in a windowless cubicle with a piano. If you scored a hit, you were moved to a cube with a window. "The competition was fierce," says King. "Don would give us an assignment: 'The Shirelles are up—they're looking for a follow-up to "Tonight's the Night."' If you didn't write it, someone else would." After a demo of "Will You Love Me Tomorrow" was completed, Kirshner played it for the Shirelles' producer, Luther Dixon, who then took it to the group. "We didn't like it at all; it sounded like a corny country and western song," says the Shirelles' Beverly Lee. "But Luther made us do it, and after he put the strings on it, we fell in love with the song."

Six weeks after its release in November 1960, the song hit the top of the charts, kick-starting the girl-group phenomenon and establishing Griffin and King as top dogs on the Brill Building's talent roster. The pair would go on to write hits for Little Eva and the Chiffons, but for Goffin, the sweetest hit was the first. "I remember Carole and Don pulled up to my lab in a limo," he says. "Carole was waving a $10,000 check, and she yelled, 'Guess what? You don't have to work anymore!'"

included Pete Seeger, whose songs about the downtrodden and politically disenfranchised were banned from the tube. Those kinds of songs might make the viewing audience feel uncomfortable and change the channel.

While *Hootenanny* attempted to strip folk music of its underlying politics, another show, *The Many Loves of Dobie Gillis*, presented Beat culture as a sort of benign adolescent style choice rather than a rebellion against the dominant culture. On the show, the character Maynard Grebs sported a sloppy beatnik style, wrinkled clothes, messy hair, and a goatee. Maynard was a character not to be taken seriously. His humorous antics on the show involved the many creative ways he avoided work. The message was that the Beats' essential trait was laziness, which was why they avoided work, not because of some exalted philosophical stance against America's values.

Beat philosophy was also trivialized with America's materialistic appropriation of its culture's most visible touchstones. By the early '60s, the rage in the suburbs was no longer backyard barbecues, but rather beatnik parties. Couples would throw parties where everyone donned berets, wore black clothes, and played bongo drums. As well, teens began setting up coffeehouses in basements and performed folk songs on acoustic guitars. In the mass culture, Beats were transformed from a threat to consumer America to a "lifestyle" that was no different from any other in the marketplace. Its products—black turtlenecks, acoustic guitars, berets—could be purchased in just about any community in America. In this way, the rebel ideas behind Beat culture were reduced to a product bought and sold in retail stores. The awesome power of America's new consumer culture could make anything—even the most radical ideas—into products to be sold.

## A BULLET TO THE HEAD

On the afternoon of November 22, 1963, whatever hope America held that everything would be okay was destroyed with one bullet. President Kennedy was assassinated in a Dallas motorcade. It was as if everyone in the country stopped and collectively held their breath. Almost every person who was old enough to remember still has that moment etched in his or her memory. "I was doing laundry when a neighbor called and told me to turn on the television," remembers one young mother. "I just sat there and watched while I held my son in my lap." Within hours, Vice President Lyndon Baines Johnson had been sworn in as the thirty-sixth president of the United States.

For the first time, an entire nation gathered in front of their television sets to witness the events unfold live. More than 100 million Americans watched John Kennedy's funeral. John-John, Kennedy's three-year-old son, stood bravely at the grave site and saluted, breaking hearts across the country. Dressed in black, Jacqueline Kennedy, the president's wife, wore a mask of grief. Hour after hour, the three television networks presented the same pictures to a mourning nation.

Perhaps prophetically, the country also witnessed Kennedy's assassin, Lee Harvey Oswald, gunned down in front of the police by Jack Ruby on November 24. This vigilante execution came to underscore the powerlessness of the government to protect us from evil. With the Cold War having been ramped up by the Cuban Missile Crisis, and with the assassination of President Kennedy, the too-short years of unlimited possibility seemed to come to an end. As historian David Farber concluded, "With his death, Americans confronted the grim reality: not all of America's possibilities were good."

"I don't know if you know how cynical most people of our generation have become about patriotism. When Kennedy spoke, he managed to instill a feeling of pride in me because I, too, was an American.... It takes a great man and now he's gone."

—Taken from one of more than 1,000,000 letters of condolence sent by Americans to Jacqueline Kennedy

# SITTING AT THE COUNTER

**A**round 4:30 p.m. on February 1, 1960, long after the lunch hour rush, Frank McCain, Junior Blair, Joe McNeil, and David Richmond sat down at the Woolworth's lunch counter in Greensboro, North Carolina. Nearly everyone gasped. One of the black waitresses motioned for the young men to leave, warning them not to sit there. The counter where they had seated themselves was reserved exclusively for whites; McCain, Blair, McNeil, and Richmond were black. No African American had ever sat at the whites-only counter before. Years later, Joe McNeil recalled that quiet winter afternoon at Woolworth's:

I don't think there's any specific reason why that particular day was chosen....But we did walk in that day...and we sat at a lunch counter where blacks never sat before. And people started to look at us. The help, many of whom were black, looked at us in disbelief too. They were concerned about our safety. We asked for service, and we were denied, and we expected to be denied. We asked why couldn't we be served, and obviously we weren't given a reasonable answer and it was our intent to sit there until they decided to serve us. We had planned to come back the following day and to repeat that scenario. Others found out what we had done, because the press became aware of what was happening. So the next day when we decided to go down again, I think we went with fifteen, and the third day it was probably a hundred and fifty, and then it probably mushroomed to a thousand or so, and then it spread to another city. All rather spontaneously, of course, and before long, I guess probably fifteen or twenty cities, and that's when we had our thing going.

## "We had our thing going."

**Woolworth's Lunch Counter in Greensboro, North Carolina**

Reporter:

# "How long have you been planning this?"

Frank McCain, Junior Blair, Joe McNeil, and David Richmond:

# "All our lives!"

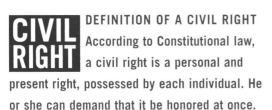

**CIVIL RIGHT**

**DEFINITION OF A CIVIL RIGHT** According to Constitutional law, a civil right is a personal and present right, possessed by each individual. He or she can demand that it be honored at once.

Within days, protests had spread across the South to fifteen cities in five states. Over the next two years, lunch counter sit-ins occurred across the South. Whites, however, reacted strongly to the protests. In Greensboro, it took seven months of sit-ins to desegregate public facilities there. In Marshall, Texas, the local authorities used fire hoses to disperse sit-in protesters. Most of the sit-ins were met with heavy resistance, with whites pouring ketchup and mustard over the heads of the protesters and committing other physical assaults. In a wade-in at a public beach in Biloxi, Mississippi, as many as ten African Americans were wounded by gunfire. In Jacksonville, Florida, a race riot erupted and at least fifty people were injured. In Atlanta, Georgia, acid was thrown in a protester's face.

In the end, more than seventeen school districts and countless stores, beaches, libraries, and movie theaters were integrated. The success of the sit-ins taught young African Americans that they did not have to wait for their elders in more established civil rights organizations such as the NAACP to take action. They did not have to wait for arduous court cases to wind their way to the Supreme Court, only to be ignored by local authorities. They didn't have to wait for big companies to see how discrimination hurt their business. They could lead the fight to end racism and discrimination with direct and immediate action.

The lunch counter sit-ins marked the first civil-rights events of the '60s. What set them apart from previous protests against segregation was that these actions occurred on a national, not just a local, level. This would make them the model for the mass protests on college campuses and around the country that would follow in the coming years.

## RACISM IN AMERICA

In America, racism has a long and varied history, and the dramatic strides against it that came in the '60s did not begin there. African Americans have been fighting racism ever since they were brought here against their will to be slaves. They fought for emancipation from slavery again and again before the Civil War. Afterward, during Reconstruction, they struggled to ensure their freedom in a country that did not truly consider them equals. They were thwarted by the government and the Supreme Court in its 1896 ruling *Plessy v. Ferguson*, which upheld "separate but equal" laws. Between Reconstruction and World War II, blacks made little measurable progress against institutional discrimination, but organizations such as the NAACP laid the groundwork for the progress that would come. During the economic boom of the '50s, blacks were able to make real strides in dismantling state-sponsored discrimination.

In 1954, the Supreme Court in its *Brown v. Board of Education* ruled that segregated schools were illegal. Chief Justice Earl Warren read the Supreme Court's ten-page unanimous decision. "We come then," the ruling read, "to the question presented: Does segregation of children in public schools solely on the basis of race, even though

"Somewhere in the universe a gear in the machinery had shifted."
—civil rights activist Eldridge Cleaver commenting on Rosa Parks's refusal to give up her seat on a Montgomery bus

# Rosa Parks

On December 1, 1955, Rosa Parks was not "moving back." She was tired. She needed to sit and she was not getting up. Parks described what happened years later:

Having to take a certain section [on the bus] because of your race was humiliating, but having to stand up because a particular driver wanted to keep a white person from having to stand was, to my mind, most inhumane.

On December 1, 1955, I had finished my day's work as a tailor's assistant in the Montgomery Fair department store and I was on my way home. There was one vacant seat on the Cleveland Avenue bus, which I took, alongside a man and two women across the aisle. There were still a few vacant seats in the white section in the front, of course. We went to the next stop without being disturbed. On the third, the front seats were occupied and this one man, a white man, was standing. The driver asked us to stand up and let him have those seats, and when none of us moved at his first words, he said, "You'll all make it light on yourselves and let me have those seats." And the man who was sitting next to the window stood up, and I made room for him to pass by me. The two women across the aisle stood up and moved out.

When the driver saw me still sitting, he asked if I was going to stand up and I said, "No, I'm not."

And he said, "Well, if you don't stand up, I'm going to call the police and have you arrested."

I said, "You may do that."

He did get off the bus, and I still stayed where I was. Two policemen came on the bus. One of the policemen asked me if the bus driver had asked me to stand and I said yes.

He said, "Why don't you stand up?"

And I asked him, "Why do you push us around?"

He said, "I do not know, but the law is the law and you're under arrest."

physical facilities and other 'tangible' factors may be equal, deprive the children of the minority group of educational opportunities? We believe it does." The ruling took only fifteen minutes to read aloud, but it would take years for it to be finally implemented. To add to the delay, a year later on May 31, 1955, the Supreme Court qualified its decision with the statement that desegregation must have "a prompt and reasonable start toward full compliance...with all deliberate speed." That phrase "with all deliberate speed" was all Southern states needed to delay implementation. "Deliberate speed" to Southern whites meant they could pretend to be moving forward without actually desegregating.

Even though the ruling was a huge success because it established the legal right to equality, the decision exposed the limits of what could be achieved through the courts if the people in charge of implementing the decision were unwilling. African Americans won in principle, but lost in implementation. Justice in the courtroom could not be translated into justice in the streets.

Parks's action sparked the entire African-American community of Montgomery to react. Beginning on December 5, more than 50,000 blacks joined a bus boycott that lasted 381 days. The bus companies, which were private, lost two thirds of their revenue and nearly went bankrupt. The Montgomery bus boycott was a success only because a federal court ruled against the city. It was also limited to the local community. It did not lead to similar boycotts across the South or change the discriminatory laws in other communities.

The protests did, however, bring to prominence Martin Luther King Jr. At the time, King was a twenty-seven-year-old minister who was new to the city, but his leadership and the principles he preached became the cornerstone of the Civil Rights Movement. In his initial address at a church in Montgomery, King said:

Now, let us say that we are not advocating violence. We have overcome that. I want it to be known throughout Montgomery and throughout the nation that we are a Christian people. **The only weapon that we have in our hands this evening is the weapon of protest.**

With these words King initiated the nonviolent tactics that would become the hallmark of the modern Civil Rights Movement. They were in stark contrast to the violence of the Ku Klux Klan, the White Citizens' Council, and other white racist organizations that tried to keep blacks "in their place."

King would go on to become the president of the Southern Christian Leadership Conference (SCLC), an organization of black ministers against segregation. The SCLC eventually would help move the Civil Rights Movement from isolated regional protests into a national movement. But that would not happen until young people involved in grassroots organizations like the Student Nonviolent Coordinating Committee incorporated King's

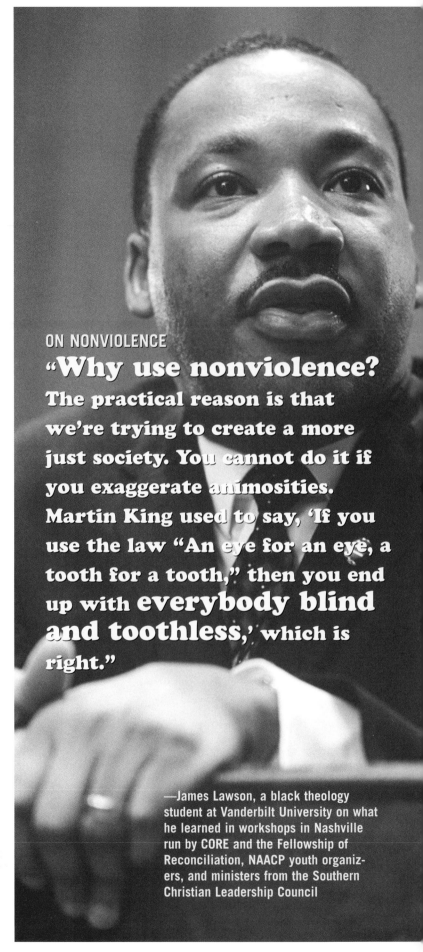

**ON NONVIOLENCE**

"**Why use nonviolence?** The practical reason is that we're trying to create a more just society. You cannot do it if you exaggerate animosities. Martin King used to say, 'If you use the law "An eye for an eye, a tooth for a tooth," then you end up with **everybody blind and toothless,**' which is right."

—James Lawson, a black theology student at Vanderbilt University on what he learned in workshops in Nashville run by CORE and the Fellowship of Reconciliation, NAACP youth organizers, and ministers from the Southern Christian Leadership Council

**When asked why he was in Little Rock, a soldier answered it was to "keep the niggers out!"**

principles to lead the way with the lunch counter sit-ins. In addition, two other important developments came out of the 1960 bus boycott. First, blacks discovered that they could exert economic pressure on corporations to end segregation, and second, the federal courts would support their efforts to end segregation. What became clear from these results was that on a national level, segregation could be fought and won. Locally, however, the effort to change these racist laws would face violent resistance.

Other events also paved the way for the lunch counter sit-ins, including the "Little Rock Nine" attempting to integrate the public schools in Little Rock, Arkansas. On September 4, 1957, nine black high school students—six girls and three boys—dared to integrate Little Rock Central High. Even though it was more than three years after the Supreme Court had ruled that black children had the right to attend white schools, no Southern school district in the deep South had yet to obey the law. Little Rock was going to be the test case. The television and print media had descended on the city to capture this historic moment. What the nation saw was the ugly face of racism. White children and parents lined the street leading to the school and hurled racial epithets at the nine African-American students. On orders from Governor Orval E. Faubus, the Alabama National Guard denied the students entrance to the school.

**The fallout from integrating Little Rock schools was that the following year, Little Rock Central High did not open at all and remained closed for the entire 1958–59 school year.**

# THE LITTLE ROCK NINE

From top left: Ernest Green, Daisy Bates (adult supporter), Carlotta Walls, Terrance Roberts, Melba Patillo, Jefferson Thomas. From bottom left: Gloria Ray, Elizabeth Eckford, Minnie Jean Brown, and Thelma Mothershed.

## THE FREEDOM RIDERS: MAY 4, 1961

"Why didn't the federal government enforce its laws?" asked James Farmer, cofounder and president of the Congress of Racial Equality (CORE). Farmer asked this question at the beginning of 1961, when the Supreme Court finally banned segregation in bus terminals, waiting areas, restaurants, and restrooms. It had been fifteen years since the 1946 Supreme Court decision against segregation on buses and trains, but African Americans were still waiting for the ruling to be enforced.

Farmer felt the time was ripe to test the resolve of the federal government. John F. Kennedy was about to be inaugurated as president of the United States. In his campaign, Kennedy had clearly spoken out in support of equal rights for African Americans. Farmer and his colleagues at CORE wanted to challenge the new Kennedy administration to back up its words with action. Farmer reasoned:

**If we were right in assuming that the federal government did not enforce federal law because of its fear of reprisals from the South, then what we had to do was make it more dangerous politically for the federal government not to enforce federal law. And how do we do that? We decided the way to do it was to have an interracial group ride through the South. This was not civil disobedience, really, because we would be doing merely what the Supreme Court said we had a right to do.**

## BACKGROUND MAP

**1961 FREEDOM RIDES**
* Violence

APRIL 22    MAY 4    MAY 17    JUNE 13    JUNE 13    JULY 8    AUG 2    NOV. 1    NOV. 29    DEC. 1

AP Newsfeatures

CORE carefully selected, recruited, and trained thirteen people—seven blacks and six whites—to exercise their civil rights on buses and in bus terminals. On May 4, they divided into two groups, one boarding a Greyhound bus and the other boarding a Trailways bus. They traveled to Richmond, Petersburg, and Lynchburg, Virginia, without incident. On May 9, however, violence erupted at the Greyhound station in Rock Hill, South Carolina. Here, black volunteer John Lewis was clubbed and beaten by whites when he tried to sit in a whites-only waiting room. Others in the group were also beaten. In the end no arrests were made and the riders were allowed into the waiting room. The riders, with others joining the protest, then proceeded to Sumter, Camden, Augusta, Athens, and Atlanta, Georgia, without incident.

On May 14, a white mob attacked both black and white freedom riders at a bus station outside of Birmingham, Alabama. Six days later the freedom riders were attacked again by a white mob of one thousand in Montgomery, Alabama, and as many as twenty-five people were injured. On May 24, more than seven freedom riders were jailed in Jackson, Mississippi, and four days later another seventeen were jailed for defying a federal injunction prohibiting their activity. Finally, Attorney General Robert Kennedy sent in U.S. marshals to Alabama to stop the violence. At the same time, the governor of Alabama declared martial law and dispatched the National Guard to calm certain areas.

At this point the Civil Rights Movement began to take on the trappings of an old-fashioned morality play. Blacks would petition the Supreme Court to secure their rights. White Southern authorities would ignore the Court's ruling. With national television and print media present, blacks would attempt to exercise their rights. White mobs would attack the black protesters to prevent them. Finally, political pressure through the national media would force the federal government to act to ensure the civil rights of all of its citizens. This drama had to be played out over and over again across the South.

## SNICK: STUDENT NONVIOLENT COORDINATING COMMITTEE

Inspired by the sit-ins and other nonviolent protests they participated in, more than 300 college students across the South met on Easter weekend of 1960 in Raleigh, North Carolina, to make a place for young people in the movement. The real question was whether to become a youth arm of the Southern Christian Leadership Conference or to form a separate group. Since many of those in attendance were critical of how the SCLC centered on Martin Luther King Jr., it was decided that they should form a more "group-centered" organization. The Student Nonviolent Coordinating Committee emerged from this meeting. Because its initials were SNCC, members quickly began referring to the group as "snick." Along with King's SCLC, the SNCC became one of the movement's most important organizations.

## THE ALBANY MOVEMENT
# November 1, 1961

"They were for freedom. I understood that, and I had been waiting," said Bernice Johnson Reagon as she summed up the feelings of the black community in Albany, Georgia. Charles Sherrod, twenty-two, and Cordell Reagon, eighteen, two young but experienced SNCC volunteers, had arrived in Terrell County during the summer to begin a voter registration drive. By the fall they moved their base to Albany. Here, Sherrod and Cordell Reagon organized nonviolence workshops in church basements. Surprisingly, the NAACP sent representatives to Albany to discourage the black community from listening to Sherrod and Reagon. They were wary of SNCC's operating independent of them. Despite this, nine students volunteered for Albany's first sit-in. The protest took place on November 1, 1961, at the local bus station. Even though no one was arrested that day, the civil action galvanized the black community there. They came together to form an organization called the Albany Movement. Its mission was to end segregation in all areas of life in the town. The Albany Movement was the largest mass protest since the Montgomery bus boycott. It exceeded the boycott, however, in its ambition because for the first time a black community was attempting to eliminate the entire system of segregation, not just one segment, such as buses.

Over the coming year, the Albany Movement introduced a new element to the civil rights struggle: mass demonstrations. Organizers led marches to the train station, to city hall, and to the courthouse. On December 16, Martin Luther King Jr. lent his name and the power of SCLC to the protests by leading a march on city hall. He and a number of other demonstrators were arrested. Sadly, the Albany city council refused to consider any demands for desegregation.

Albany's white police chief, Laurie Pritchett, had perhaps the most unique response to the protests. He had researched nonviolent protests and understood that meeting them with violence would make the protesters heroes.

As a result, Chief Pritchett would kindly bow his head in prayer as he arrested black ministers.

Without violence, the ugly face of racism could not be splashed across the nation's television screens and newspapers. Without violence, the federal government felt no pressure to intervene. In fact, the Kennedy administration complimented Albany's segregationists for their restraint. The result of Pritchett's restraint and the city's refusal even to consider desegregating was a serious blow to the Movement. As the protests sputtered along for months, black leaders began to blame each other for the failure. The infighting became so tense that the once-united organizations involved—SNCC, King's SCLC, the NAACP—began to splinter. "We're tired, very tired. I'm tired. We're sick of it," Martin Luther King Jr. said to Attorney General Robert Kennedy afterward.

James Meredith escorted by U.S. marshals

*freedom*

## JAMES MEREDITH INTEGRATES OLE MISS
# September 30, 1962

One hundred twenty-three deputy federal marshals.

Three hundred sixteen U.S. border patrolmen.

Ninety-seven federal prison guards.

That is what it took to enroll one black student into the University of Mississippi, "Ole Miss." At six p.m. on Sunday, September 30, James Meredith was flown to Oxford, Mississippi, and secretly escorted onto campus. Within the hour, more than 2,000 protesters attacked Meredith's protectors. Ordered not to shoot back, the U.S. marshals were assaulted throughout the night by guns, bottles, bricks, Molotov cocktails, and a bulldozer. The marshals fought back with tear gas. At six a.m. the next morn-ing, federal troops arrived and pushed the mob back into the town square. By eight a.m., when Meredith officially registered for school, 28 marshals had been shot and 160 injured.

After two years at Jackson State College, James Meredith had transferred to Ole Miss. After another year and much protest, he graduated on August 18, 1963.

"What really happened in the Meredith case when the state decided to resist was that they were playing out the last chapter of the Civil War."

—Constance Baker Motley, an attorney for the NAACP Legal Defense Fund and James Meredith's attorney

## MARCHING IN BOMBINGHAM
# April 12, 1963

"Birmingham is where it's at, gentlemen," said Fred Shuttlesworth, minister at Birmingham's Bethel Baptist Church and a cofounder of the SCLC. "I assure you, if you come to Birmingham, we will not only gain prestige but really shake the country. If you win in Birmingham, as Birmingham goes, so goes the nation."

Martin Luther King Jr. and the SCLC listened to Shuttlesworth and came. After the failure of Albany, it was clear to everyone in the Civil Rights Movement that the only way to get progress was to provoke aggression from the segregationists in front of the media. The mass marketplace had become so powerful that national media now influenced local politics.

SCLC came up with a plan to tap just that power. It was called Project C. Its aim was to provoke segregationists into violent acts that would force the entire nation to face the evil of segregation. On April 12, Good Friday, Martin Luther King Jr., Ralph Abernathy, and Fred Shuttlesworth led a group of fifty protesters out of church. They marched to city hall, where they were promptly arrested. King's arrest made the front page of the *New York Times*. No sooner was this group incarcerated than another took to the streets to protest their arrest. This continued day after day until King and the others were released a week later.

King then opened the second phase of his

**Civil Rights protesters marching in Birmingham**

NO MORE BIRMINGHAMS

While in jail, King wrote his now legendary "Letter from Birmingham Jail," which was a statement of purpose for the Civil Rights Movement. Here is an excerpt:

You may well ask: "Why direct action? Why sit-ins, marches, and so forth? Isn't negotiating a better path?" You are quite right in calling for negotiation. Indeed, this is the very purpose of direct action. Nonviolent direct action seeks to create such a crisis and foster such a tension that a community which has constantly refused to negotiate is forced to confront the issue. It seeks so to dramatize the issue that it can no longer be ignored.... So must we see the need for nonviolent gadflies to create the kind of tension in society that will help men rise from the dark depths of prejudice and racism to the majestic heights of understanding and brotherhood....

campaign. He spent two weeks recruiting children ages six to sixteen to march. This was the biggest risk of his career. If any of these children were hurt by the snapping police dogs or fire hoses so powerful they could strip bark from a tree, King would be held responsible. Over this period, volunteers trained the children to protect their heads, eyes, and genitals, and they taught the children the principles of nonviolent protest.

On May 2, hundreds of kids filed out of the Sixteenth Street Baptist Church singing "We Shall Overcome." The police arrested the children by the dozen, by the score, and finally by the hundreds. By nightfall there were 959 children in the Birmingham jail. The next day all hell broke loose. The city commissioner in charge of the police, Eugene "Bull" Connor, set up ambushes in preparation for the protesters. The jail was full so Connor decided to prevent blacks from protesting by using extreme measures. The police refused to allow five hundred black protesters to leave the church. In the streets, they clubbed black pro-

**Wreckage of a bomb exploded near King's motel in Birmingham**

Inside the grounds of the Birmingham jail the children were forced to stand for hours in the rain. Other children were given strong laxatives and placed in cells with no toilets. Girls were forced to scrub the dirty jail floors with tooth-brushes.

testers, savaged them with dogs, and sprayed fire hoses at them. Children were sent spinning down the street by the bursts of water. Others were beaten to the ground.

Television cameras recorded for the nation white men, their faces flushed and twisted into expressions of hatred, zealously attacking unarmed children and adults.

Now phase three was launched. King sent thousands of protesters into the streets. Heavily outnumbered, the Birmingham police lashed out with renewed fury. The city became a bloodbath. Connor realized the protests were beyond his control and called Governor George Wallace, who sent almost the entire Alabama state police. At this point the Justice Department was forced to step in and persuade local business leaders to use their influence on the city's white establishment. Robert Kennedy contacted

King and asked him to accept this chance to negotiate. A four-point peace agreement was hammered out:

1. Customers' restrooms in downtown stores were desegregated.
2. The stores would hire black sales assistants and clerks.
3. All jailed demonstrators were to be released.
4. Biracial committees were created to remedy black grievances.

Despite this agreement, Birmingham was to descend into more violence. The home of King's brother and the A. G. Gaston Motel were bombed in an attempt to assassinate King. Neither bombings injured anyone, but in response, blacks rioted in the streets, smashing store windows and setting fire to parked cars. Peace eventually was restored, but Birmingham would remain a dangerous place for months to come.

## THE MARCH ON WASHINGTON
# August 28, 1963

When more than 250,000 marchers descended on the nation's capital chanting, "Pass that bill! Pass that bill! Pass that bill!" veteran civil rights activist A. Philip Randolph's dream had finally come true. As the gray wise man of the Movement at seventy-four, Randolph first proposed the march in 1940. Twenty-three years later, when Bayard Rustin suggested that now was the time, Randolph heartily agreed. On the hot, humid day of August 28, Randolph and Rustin led a massive march onto the National Mall in front of the Lincoln Memorial. The event was called the March on Washington for Jobs and Freedom and was meant to pressure the president to push through Congress his bill to "make a commitment it has not fully made in this century to the population that race has no place in American life or law." Blacks called this bill the "Second Emancipation Proclamation," referring to Lincoln's proclamation to free the slaves exactly one hundred years before. This proclamation was meant to finish what Lincoln had begun.

From the steps of the Lincoln Memorial, major figures from every branch of the Civil Rights Movement spoke to the crowd. There were performances by gospel singer Mahalia Jackson and folksingers Joan Baez and Bob Dylan. Despite the sense of unity in the crowd, behind the scenes the struggle between the younger generation and the Movement's older, more conservative leaders threatened to split them. SNCC chairman John Lewis planned to deliver an impassioned speech that included a threat that the Movement would "march through the heart of Dixie, the way Sherman did," referring to the Union general who burned his way through the South. This rift was one of the first clear signs that the younger leaders were becoming impatient with the movement's strategy of nonviolence and negotiation. In the end Lewis backed down, but this would not be the case in the future.

Despite this tension, the march's crowning moment was when Martin Luther King Jr. stepped up to the podium. He began slowly and bitterly, "There will be neither rest nor tranquility in America until the Negro is granted his citizenship rights. The whirlwinds of revolt will continue to shake the foundations of our nation until the bright day of justice emerges." As King paused and looked out at the crowd, he realized their mood was joyous, and did not match the solemnity of his prepared speech. Instead, he launched into a speech that he had been polishing and practicing before church groups and community groups for years. "I have a dream that my four little children will one day live in a nation where they will not be judged by the color of their skin, but by the content of their character. I have a dream today!" The cadence of his repeated "I have a dream" statement inspired the crowd and the nation. It became the keynote refrain for the Civil Rights Movement.

The March on Washington for Jobs and Freedom was the first mass protest march on the capital and set the stage for many more to come in the next decade. This mass march would become the standard that other groups would use to lobby for their goals.

## THE BIRMINGHAM CHURCH BOMBING
# September 15, 1963

Just over two weeks later, Birmingham would once again be in the nation's headlines. Shortly before 10:30 a.m. on Sunday, September 15, a bomb exploded at one of the most active churches in the city. The explosion rocked the building. Walls and ceilings collapsed. Lying among the rubble were twenty injured black children. Four little girls—Addie May Collins, Denise McNair, Carole Robertson, and Cynthia Wesley—were dead. Within hours African Americans were rioting in the streets, clashing with crowds of working-class whites. The police were able to clear the streets, but not before two more black youths were killed.

The bombing of the Sunday school was the fifty-first racial bombing in Birmingham since 1946. Not one of the

"I have a dream that my four little children will one day live in a nation where they will not be judged by the color of their skin, but by the content of their character. I have a dream today"

Since 1947, more than thirty bombs had gone off in Birmingham, causing blacks to refer to the city as both "Tragic City" and "Bombingham."

Between 1956 and 1963, not a single month passed without a racial bombing in the eleven states of the Old Confederacy.

preceding fifty blasts had led to an arrest and conviction. The two white men who perpetrated this bombing were arrested and then released.

## THE SECOND EMANCIPATION PROCLAMATION
# July 2, 1964

"We are confronted primarily with a moral issue. It is as old as the Scriptures and is as clear as the American Constitution. The heart of the question is whether all Americans can be afforded equal rights and equal opportunities, whether we are going to treat our fellow Americans as we want to be treated...."

President Kennedy spoke these words in a televised speech on the evening of June 11, 1963. Earlier in the day, Alabama Governor George Wallace "stood at the schoolhouse door" and refused admission to a black student. Later that night after Kennedy's speech, Medgar Evers, the first full-time representative of the NAACP in Mississippi, would return home after watching Kennedy's speech and be assassinated on his doorstep in front of his wife and children. Evers had devoted his life to the Civil Rights Movement. He had gained national attention for his investigations into violent crimes against blacks and had led a boycott against Jackson, Mississippi, merchants.

Kennedy's speech marked a change in the federal government's resolve to enforce equal rights for black Americans, but Kennedy would not live to see his civil rights legislation signed into law. After his assassination, the newly sworn-in president, Lyndon Baines Johnson, would make it his mission to ensure Kennedy's legacy. At the top of that list was Kennedy's Civil Rights Act. In his first address to Congress, Johnson said, "First, no memorial or eulogy could more eloquently honor President Kennedy's memory than the earliest possible passage of the civil rights bill for which he fought so long. We have talked enough in this country about equal rights. We have talked for one hundred years or more. It's time now to write the next chapter, and to write it in the books of law."

On July 2, the historic 1964 Civil Rights Act finally passed Congress, despite heavy opposition by Southern Democrats. The act changed the country in fundamental ways. In addition to attacking racial discrimination, it tore down America's long-standing tradition of second-class citizenship for women. It outlawed job discrimination based on race or gender. It outlawed discrimination in all public accommodations, including restaurants, hotels, waiting rooms, and theaters. It prohibited the federal government from funding any program at the national, state, or local level that discriminated. The Justice Department was given greater powers to fight against school discrimination, and a new federal agency, the Equal Employment Opportunity Commission, was created to fight employers who practiced discrimination.

The Civil Rights Movement, almost a century after the end of the Civil War, finally succeeded in enlisting the federal government in the fight against racial injustice. Then, virtually on their own, a block of moderate Democrat and Republican congressmen extended that fight to include justice for women as well.

Clearly, for those involved in the Movement at the time, the Civil Rights Act of 1964 appeared to be the answer to achieving racial justice in America.

For the Boomer Generation that was just coming of age, the lessons from the successes *and* failures of the Civil Rights Movement were just the beginning.

"I draw the line in the dust and toss the gauntlet before the feet of tyranny and I say **segregation now... Segregation tomorrow... Segregation forever.**"

—George C. Wallace (pictured standing at the schoolhouse door) in his inaugural address upon becoming governor of Alabama on January 14, 1963

"You never forget what poverty and hatred can do when you see its scars on the face of a young child."

—President Johnson on his reasons for supporting civil rights

# YOU SAY YOU WANT A REVOLUTION

## THE RADICAL YOUTH MOVEMENT

## NEW GENERATION NOW

**"We're more popular than Jesus."**
**— John Lennon of the Beatles, 1966**

That's the way it felt, not just for Lennon and the Beatles, but for everyone who grew up in the '60s. The '50s had taught them day in and day out that as children they were the center of the universe, at least in America. The result of this unheard-of attention was the largest generation of teenagers with an inevitable sense of entitlement. Boomers not only felt pride in their domination, but that satisfaction often tipped into an inflated sense of importance.

Their dominance easily led to a logical fallacy: Since the American economy was driven by their whims and desires, then the country as a whole should be driven by the opinions and ideas of these adolescents. Whether that arrogance would intensify into the kind of hubris of ancient tragedy, however, would not be determined until the end of the decade. For now, it simply manifested in a confidence that they could make the world into whatever they desired.

The Beatles arrived on the scene in the wake of the Kennedy assassination. The country was in crisis. More specifically, the youth of America felt a sense of alienation and disappointment in their authority figures. Not only had they lost a president who had given them hope, but the nation had just come out of the Cuban Missile Crisis, where nuclear weapons had very nearly been pointed at it. Simultaneously, President Johnson was escalating the troop commitment to a war in Vietnam, a place nobody could even find on a map. That meant that Boomers were being drafted to fight in a conflict that they did not understand and were not remotely committed to. For many of the white middle-class teens going off to college, it seemed as though everything their parents had preached about—conformity buying contentment—could not protect them from nuclear threats and death in a jungle on the other side of the world.

Besides these external anxieties, the country was witnessing real, concrete evil from within. Each night television stations reported on white racists denying civil rights to African Americans and attacking, even murdering,

songs. "They broke out of three-chord rock and four-chord teenybop," writes Lennon biographer Jon Wiener. More specifically, they brought unpredictable twists to a music genre that had become incredibly predictable. Both Lennon and McCartney were self-made musicians who did not know how to read music and refused to learn. Their compositions contained none of the preconceived notions about what chord follows another. Instead, they were open to exploit whatever sounded good to them: beginning and ending songs in the wrong key, employing modal, pentatonic, and Indian scales, incorporating studio effects and exotic instruments, and shuffling rhythms and idioms. As the decade progressed, they experimented with

# The Beatles embodied the generation gap—they launched a new era of independent singer-songwriters delivering their own messages.

those who stood up to protest. The utopian world of plenitude and suburban bliss was simply a thin veneer that was quickly cracking. It was at this point that the "generation gap" really became apparent. Because their parents' generation was so intent on protecting the status quo, teens and young adults were quickly becoming skeptical of the values they had been raised on.

John, Paul, George, and Ringo—the Fab Four—arrived at just the right time. Their innovative combination of African-American R&B with their own brilliant and intuitive song composition returned rock-and-roll to its roots, which surprisingly had been lost over the previous five years. Hit factories like the Brill Building moved away from rock's African-American origins toward bubblegum pop written by professionals and performed by groups created by record labels.

The Beatles, despite performing songs on similar topics, launched a new era of performers who sang their own

everything from tape loops to drugs to chance techniques borrowed from the intellectual avant-garde.

From the beginning, the Fab Four tapped into the burgeoning mass culture and used it for their own ends. Rather than reinforcing parental conformity as the path to contentment, John, Paul, George, and Ringo keyed into the mass consumption notions of the new always being better, and the *new* became anything white suburban America had never experienced—namely working-class England and black America. The Beatles also introduced a whole generation of Boomers to the Beat sensibility of a reverence for the margins of American culture. In this way the Beatles were able to tap into the mass market and deliver their own message to the masses without intervention from authority figures.

Where that message would take them was not yet clear. What was clear was the reality that the competing values of restraint and instant gratification could not be resolved.

Something new had to replace it. Kennedy's vision of a New Frontier had clearly not worked. His assassination and the Vietnam War escalation would demonstrate this. In the coming years, Boomers would find themselves being pulled to one pole or the other. Both directions meant to change the world and create the utopia they had been promised as children. One direction was defined by nineteenth-century values of hard work and seriousness, the other by pleasure and hedonism. One would embrace political radicalism, the other cultural radicalism.

## BRINGING DOWN THE SYSTEM

> You say you want a revolution
> Well, you know
> we all want to change the world.
> —*"Revolution," the Beatles*

It was as if they could read the future. By June of 1966,

the Beatles had dropped their "Yeah Yeah" sound and put out a record of startling originality, *Yesterday and Today*. Even the cover displayed a more radical and edgy look. On it, the mop tops had cast aside their cute pop look and replaced it with a gruesome photo of them dressed in bloody butchers' aprons wielding knives and accompanied by a box of sausages, a plate of raw meat, two hundred nails, and dismembered heads of baby dolls. Response to the cover photo by retailers was immediate. Stores refused to carry the album. Capitol Records had to recall them and glue a bland stock photo of the band on the album sleeve.

With this album, the Beatles were radicalized. "The cover was as relevant as the Vietnam War," argued John Lennon. "If the public could accept something as cruel as the war, then they could accept that cover." By the spring of the next year, the Beatles weren't alone in their opposition to the war.

**Sixties protest poster**

"Hell, no! We won't go!" became the catchphrase of Vietnam War protesters on campuses across the country. On April 14, 1967, thousands of angry screaming young people marched through Manhattan and San Francisco. They shouted "Hell, no! We won't go!" "Hey, hey, LBJ! How many kids did you kill today?" and "Ho Ho Ho Chi Minh! The Vietcong are going to win!" Inspired by the 1963 civil rights March on Washington, these mass demonstrations, attracting more than 250,000 participants, were organized by a broad-based coalition of non-radical, nonmilitant protesters who wanted to force President Johnson to negotiate a peaceful withdrawal of American troops from Vietnam. Surprisingly, they were joined by religious leaders, mothers, and many others, including respectable mainstream groups:

- Clergy and Laity Concerned About Vietnam
- Business Executives Move for a Vietnam Peace
- Washington Physicians and Other Health Workers for Peace in Vietnam
- Returnees Association (ex–Peace Corps volunteers)
- Federation of American Scientists
- International Ladies' Garment Workers Union
- Americans for Democratic Action
- a group of Rhodes Scholars
- Another Mother for Peace

By 1967, the majority of Americans were moving slowly from unquestioning support of the war to leaning against American involvement. One of the most dramatic and emblematic shifts was Jane Fonda's position on war. In 1962, the Pentagon's official designation for Fonda was "Miss Army Recruiting." By 1972, after visiting North Vietnam, her unofficial sobriquet became "Hanoi Jane," which derisively noted her support of the Communist regime the American troops were fighting.

The extraordinary swing to opposing the war began, however, not as a mainstream movement, but as an out-cropping of a small, leftist student organization, Students for a Democratic Society (SDS). Though SDS was not primarily anti-Vietnam, they saw the escalation of the Vietnam War as a symptom of a much larger problem in America and thus a good place to focus their initial energy. When SDS met at Port Huron, Michigan, in June of 1962 after the spring semester had ended, the members were inspired by the democratic principles of the Student Nonviolent Coordinating Committee (SNCC), which had been so successful in organizing the lunch counter sit-ins and later the Freedom Summer in 1964. Like the SNCC, these college students wanted to address what they saw as the biggest problems in America. In their "Port Huron Statement," they wrote:

ANOTHER MOTHER FOR PEACE.

We are people of this generation, bred in at least modest comfort, housed now in universities, looking uncomfortably to the world we inherit.... **Many of us began maturing in complacency.** As we grew, however, our comfort was penetrated by events too troubling to dismiss. First, the permeating and victimizing fact of human degradation, symbolized by the Southern struggle against racial bigotry, **compelled most of us from silence to activism.** Second, the enclosing fact of the Cold War, symbolized by the presence of the Bomb, brought awareness that we...might die at any time. We might deliberately ignore, or avoid, or fail to feel all other human problems, but not these two.

SDS saw their organization as the future of the left wing in this country. The "Old Left" was still reeling from the McCarthy era, which had marginalized left-thinking intellectuals as Communist sympathizers. At the time of the Port Huron meeting the only real left were the labor unions that were rigidly anti-Communist. SDS wanted to lead the country into an era of the "New Left" made up of students and a new generation of youths. They saw their mission as returning democracy to the people. In their view, America was being controlled by what radical sociologist C. Wright Mills called the "power elite," composed of "upper circles of the corporate, political, and military worlds."

This elite was referred to by a number of names, including the "military-industrial complex," "the system," "the machine," and simply "the man." The New Left saw this elite as interested almost exclusively in promoting their own interests and maintaining power. From the New Left's perspective, the consequences of "the system's" hunger for control was leading America into a spiraling arms race, a hysterical Cold War standoff, and a system of fundamental economic inequality, all of which SDS found reprehensible.

How many kids did you kill today?"

"HO HO HO CHI MINH! THE VIETCONG ARE GOING TO WIN! HO HO HO CHI MINH! THE VIETCONG ARE GOING TO WIN! HO HO HO CHI MINH! THE VIETCONG ARE GOING TO WIN!

"Hey, hey, LBJ! How many kids did you kill today?"

Taking a page from SNCC, SDS organized the Economic Research and Action Project in urban ghettos to help the nation's poor. The project was an unmitigated failure, except for one thing. Like SNCC's Freedom Summer, the experience of being exposed to poor black neighborhoods changed these white middle-class college students. After growing up in sheltered suburbs, the shock of the "real America" they saw led many to embrace a radical solution to poverty. They concluded that the entire capitalistic system was sick and had to be destroyed.

By 1965, SDS turned its attention to the government's escalating involvement in Vietnam. Though the government refused to call it a war, the American public knew what it meant that the U.S. military was supporting South Vietnam against the Vietcong rebels and North Vietnamese troops. It was a war, just like the Korean War a decade earlier. For members of SDS, the war seemed to be at the core of everything wrong with the country. It was the will of the nation's "power elite," not the will of the people.

While SDS was moving toward organizing a major Vietnam War protest in Washington, D.C., for the upcoming spring, out West at the University of California at Berkeley, students were organizing for a different reason. During the fall semester of 1964, college administrators banned civil rights groups from recruiting workers for civil rights organizations' Mississippi projects along Telegraph Avenue. Traditionally, this location had been where groups set up tables to distribute information. Most organizations ignored the ban, but when five students were called before the disciplinary committee for breaking the new rule, hundreds showed up and demanded to be punished as well. By October 1, the confrontation had escalated out of control when the administration ordered a CORE (Congress of Racial Equality) worker arrested and the removal of tables set up in front of the main administration building. Students spontaneously surrounded the police car. A standoff ensued with more than 4,000 students joining in the protest.

Afterward, the two most prominent political groups on campus, the Young Republicans and the SNCC, created the Free Speech Movement (FSM). This coming together of diverging political positions became a hallmark of much of the student demonstrations. Like SDS's march on Washington, the FSM believed in nonexclusion, self-determination, and mass action. A student sit-in and rally was organized for December 2. Mario Salvio, one of the leaders of FSM, addressed thousands of rallying students:

**There is a time when the operations of the machine becomes so odious, makes you so sick at heart, that you can't take part; you can't even passively take part, and you've got to put your bodies upon the gears and upon the wheels, upon the levers, upon all the apparatus and you've got to make it stop.** And you've got to indicate to the people who run it, to the people that own it, that unless you're free, the machines will be prevented from working at all.

Joan Baez followed Salvio with Dylan's generational anthem "The Times They Are A-Changin'." The rally ended with everyone singing the civil rights anthem "We Shall Overcome." Shocked by this student outburst of rebellion, the administration responded aggressively and called in the Berkeley police, who arrested 773 students. Outraged by the authorities' high-handed actions, a student strike immediately followed. Eventually, the administration caved to their demands. The movement won concessions that allowed political speech on Telegraph Avenue. Berkeley historian W. J. Rorabaught observed that the FSM "led many students to challenge the status quo.... They became feisty and contentious.... The Free Speech Movement unleashed a restless proving of life."

Within months, students and faculty were beginning to mobilize for their rights and their beliefs on campuses across the nation. In March of 1965, faculty and graduate students at the University of Michigan organized the first teach-in on the Vietnam War. The premise of the teach-in was for professors, instructors, and students to share information, argue, and discuss the war. The importance of this was that participants no longer trusted what the government or the mass media were saying about America's role in Vietnam. They took on the responsibility of educating themselves.

One month later, on April 17, 1965, SDS led a group of fringe organizations, including Quakers, pacifists, and leftists, in a protest march on the grounds of the Washington Monument, trying to emulate the 1963 Civil Rights March on Washington. Though Vietnam, with just over 40,000 troops deployed, was still barely on the radar for most Americans, SDS and the other groups—more than 25,000 participants—wanted to draw attention to the military's increasing involvement. In his speech to the crowd, Paul Potter, the president of SDS, linked the war in Vietnam to larger problems in American society. He told the gathering that something had gone wrong with America. The war in Vietnam was a sign of a failure of democracy because it benefited the interests of "the system" at the expense of the lives of the youths who were being killed. In a country that had not come to a democrat-

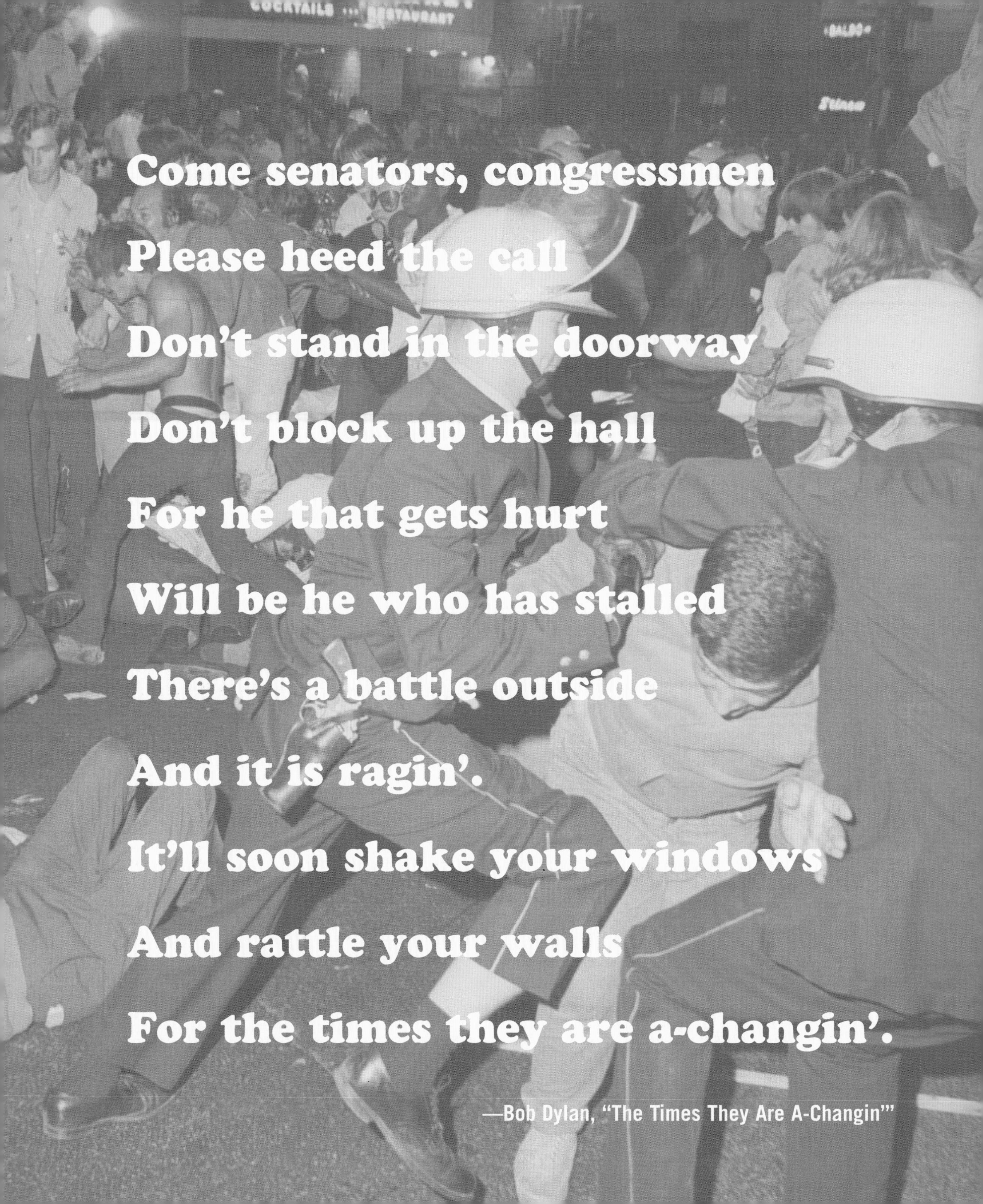

Come senators, congressmen

Please heed the call

Don't stand in the doorway

Don't block up the hall

For he that gets hurt

Will be he who has stalled

There's a battle outside

And it is ragin'.

It'll soon shake your windows

And rattle your walls

For the times they are a-changin'.

—Bob Dylan, "The Times They Are A-Changin'"

ic consensus to go to war, but had just accepted the government's decision to do so, it was imperative that a real consensus—a Movement—now form. The individuals who made up that movement had to be ready to accept the consequences of going against their government and the status quo. At the rally, Potter said:

> To build a movement rather than a protest or some series of protests, **to break out of our insulations and accept the consequences of our decisions,** in effect to change our lives, means that we can open ourselves to the reactions of a society that believes that it is moral and just, that we open ourselves to libeling and persecution, that we dare to be really seen as wrong in a society that doesn't tolerate fundamental challenges.... **All our lives, our destinies, our very hopes to live, depend on our ability to overcome that system.**

By late 1965, the protests against the war began to pick up. About 120 colleges and universities held teach-ins. Like the sit-in movement five years earlier, the teach-ins showed young people that they no longer needed simply to accept what they were told by people in authority. They could question, they could challenge, and they could act. Highlights included a national teach-in in Washington that was broadcast to 100,000 students on 100 campuses; a thirty-four-hour marathon teach-in in Berkeley, attended by 15,000; and local demonstrations on the International Days of Protest in October. From this moment forward, campuses became the center of anti–Vietnam War protests.

One of the many ironies that would arise amid this movement was the fact that parents were sending their sons and daughters to college to help them succeed within the system and continue the prosperity. While at college, these same students were introduced by their professors and instructors to the very principles of questioning the system. This was particularly true in respect to Vietnam. At the same time, college campuses became havens for young men to avoid the draft. Any full-time male college student received an automatic deferment from the draft. As a result, actions to secure the future of the establishment actually undermined it.

SDS quickly became the leader in the Anti-War Movement. Chapters began sprouting up on nearly every campus in the country, and by 1968, the organization had more than 40,000 members. Despite the success of SDS in holding the largest peace demonstration up to that point in American history, and despite the growing concern of draft-age men about the war, the organization began to back away from its leadership role in the Anti-War Movement. Its leaders were more concerned with broader ideological issues and believed that protesting against the war would only divert attention from the greater sickness in American culture. This decision proved to be a major miscalculation. The vast majority of young people in America were more concerned with losing their lives in Vietnam than with changing any system.

In some ways, SDS was correct in its self-analysis. The threat that someone from the Boomer Generation would be drafted and sent to Vietnam was small. During the war, one third of the soldiers in Vietnam had been drafted. The rest were volunteers. In addition, there was a myriad of ways in which to avoid the draft, one of which was to stay in school. Nevertheless, for young people coming of age during this time, even the likelihood of being drafted was sufficient to make their concern primary. Few really believed that the spread of Communism in that tiny country, no larger than the state of New Jersey, would truly be a threat to America. They had been brought up to cherish individual fulfillment. Fighting an unknown enemy in Asia did not fit that criterion.

The process of building anti-war actions led to the creation of broad-based local anti-war coalitions. Two areas

# ...the greatest purveyor of violence in the world today—my own government.
—Martin Luther King Jr.

of focus came out of the March on Washington and the teach-ins: First, a national coalition needed to be formed to coordinate protests; and second, the immediate withdrawal of U.S. troops from Vietnam was essential.

Between 1965 and 1968, protesters raised the level of confrontation with the "war makers." In mid-1965, protesters burned their draft cards and Congress made it a crime. By the next year, returning soldiers joined the Movement, and the first organized campus protests took place against Dow Chemical, the maker of napalm, an incendiary substance used to burn down the jungles of Vietnam but that also served to burn the flesh off victims. The New York Fifth Avenue Vietnam Peace Parade Committee, which brought hundreds of organizations together for demonstrations, led a major anti-war parade in Manhattan. At the same time, the Vietnam Day Committee—composed of free-speech activists, pacifists, and other radicals—attempted to shut down the Oakland Army Terminal, a departure point for men and matériel going to Vietnam.

By the end of the year, the Parade Committee and its partners formed the National Mobilization Committee to End the War in Vietnam (MOBE). On April 15, 1967, 500,000 people marched in the streets in New York and San Francisco in what was called the Spring Mobilization to End the War in Vietnam. At the New York rally, Martin Luther King Jr. spoke out for the first time on a non–civil rights issue.

I could never again raise my voice against the violence of the oppressed in the ghetto without having first spoken out clearly to the greatest purveyor of violence in the world today—my own government. We are at a moment when our lives must be placed on the line if our nation is to survive its own folly. Every man of humane convictions must decide on the protest that best suits his convictions, but we must all protest....I oppose the war in Vietnam because I love America. I speak out against it not in anger but with anxiety and sorrow in my heart....This war is a blasphemy against all that America stands for.

Around the same time, the editorial page of the *New York Times*, one of the country's most respected newspapers, turned against the war. On October 21, 1967, 150,000 marched on Washington in a direct political confrontation with the Pentagon and President Johnson's war policy. The leaders of this march were two counterculture jesters, Jerry Rubin and Abbie Hoffman. In the coming year, they would make headlines for their antics and the organization of the Yippies! (As in Youth International Party—with an emphasis on "party" and the exclamation point intended.) Rubin and Hoffman's rise to leadership marked a shift in the movement from one of hope to the beginnings of cynicism, as they brought a gallows humor to the movement that reflected the growing sense of futility that many radicals felt. With the government clearly not changing its policies, many were beginning to conclude that only desperate measures would force change.

Despite all of these marches and protests, the Johnson Administration was unresponsive. This wasn't a war President Johnson wanted. He'd inherited it from Kennedy, and he was not going to be the first American president to lose a war. The administration continued to increase America's involvement in Vietnam despite a shift in its policy from protecting the world against Communism to simply trying to save face. According to Assistant Secretary of Defense John McNaughton, by 1965 the main goal of U.S. policy in Vietnam was to "avoid a humiliating U.S. defeat." This meant propping up the corrupt South Vietnamese government. For America, one of the world's superpowers, to lose a war in a tiny country like Vietnam was unfathomable and had to be resisted at almost any cost. Protests from a minority of the American population were not going to change this emotion-based, rather than strategic, policy.

The growing frustration by protesters began to push many of their leaders toward radical responses—"from protest to resistance." The thinking was that if the government would not respond to peaceful demonstrations, then they would certainly respond to violence. Most of those who were becoming radicalized were making connections, like the SDS had done, between Vietnam and greater domestic and international policies of the U.S. government. This expansion of their complaints against Vietnam to broader, more general issues allowed many to become "radicalized."

### REVOLUTION ON THE MIND

And it's one, two, three, what are we fighting for?
Don't ask me, I don't give a damn
Next stop, VIETNAM!
And it's five, six, seven, open those pearly gates
Ah, there ain't no time to wonder why
Whoopee! We're all goin' to die!
—"I-Feel-Like-I'm-Fixin'-to-Die Rag,"
Country Joe and the Fish

By 1968, the Anti-War Movement began to pitch the country into a war with itself, though the majority would not turn against the Vietnam War until President Richard Nixon invaded Cambodia in 1971. A number of events conspired to tear the country apart.

The year began with a disastrous setback in Vietnam. On January 30, at the start of Tet, the lunar New Year, more than 80,000 Vietcong and North

## WHO WERE THE RADICALS?
**Most of the extreme radicals came from white middle-class backgrounds. They were honor roll students with liberal arts majors. They were also used to being listened to and having their opinions count. In the mass market, their voice and buying power drove many aspects of the economy, particularly popular culture. To have authority figures not respond to their concerns, when that had become their right, truly seemed outrageous.**

**Abbie Hoffman**

## RADICALS ON THE
## FBI MOST-WANTED LIST
*More than two dozen radicals went underground to escape arrest, but these five were notable for making the FBI's Most-Wanted List:*

**CAMERON DAVID BISHOP**, student activist at Colorado State University, blew up four power transmission line towers in 1969 to cut the supply of power to defense plants.

**ANGELA DAVIS** (below), a black activist and Communist Party member, arrested in 1970, who was acquitted in a kidnapping, murder, and conspiracy trial for a courthouse shootout.

**LAWRENCE ROBERT PLAMONDON**, founding member of the White Panther Party. Wanted for bombing a CIA recruiting office in Michigan. Arrested in Michigan but case dismissed because of illegal FBI wiretaps.

**BERNARDINE DOHRN**, a leader of Weatherman Underground, wanted for rioting, mob action, and conspiracy. Spent a decade living as a fugitive. Surrendered and was fined $1,500 and placed on probation for five years.

**LEO BURT**, student activist and accused of bombing the Army Mathematics Research Center at the University of Wisconsin-Madison, killing a researcher. Still on the lam.

## THE VIETNAM WAR BY THE NUMBERS

In 1961, the United States had 3,200 military advisers in Vietnam; in 1963, Kennedy increased that number to 16,300, which was still a small and rather insignificant number. By 1964, Johnson had increased that number by almost half to 23,300 American troops, still supposedly acting only as advisers. As the reality of the strong resistance of the Vietcong and the North Vietnamese Army became clear, Johnson became even more committed to ensuring South Vietnam's success and inserted 184,000 American troops to assist in fighting the enemy. By now Johnson had committed so many troops to the region and risked America's prestige with the world to such an extent that it became impossible for him to withdraw. Withdrawing would be a humiliation not only for the country but for Johnson personally. With this in mind, over the next three years the president escalated America's involvement to more than 550,000 U.S. troops on the ground. By the end of 1968, 30,610 American servicemen had been killed in action. When U.S. troops were finally evacuated from Vietnam in 1973, over two million American fighting men had served in the war. During that time, the war spread from Vietnam into Cambodia and Laos. Hundreds of thousands of Vietnamese, Cambodian, and Laotian people were killed. Over seven million tons of bombs were dropped, with four million tons falling on South Vietnam, an area smaller than the state of New Jersey. In all of World War II, the United States dropped two million tons of bombs and munitions over all of Europe and the Pacific. Many of the bombs dropped on Vietnam are still there, unexploded, while land mines litter the landscape, still claiming victims to this day.

Vietnamese soldiers invaded more than 100 South Vietnamese cities and towns and attacked the U.S. Embassy in Saigon. The Communist troops slaughtered thousands of Vietnamese despite the fact that the offensive lasted only one day. The surprise and effectiveness of the attack was a psychological blow to America. For months in military briefings, the government had been saying there was "light at the end of the tunnel." They led the country to believe that the enemy was incapable of a major offensive and that after some mopping up, the U.S. troops would be home. The Tet Offensive showed that the enemy was clearly not as weak as the government had been portraying it to be; in fact, just the opposite seemed true. The Communists appeared ready to continue fighting for a very long time. The Pentagon had lied to the American people by implying that victory was imminent. The end of the Vietnam War was nowhere near.

"Half a million American soldiers with 700,000 Vietnamese allies, with total command of the air, total command of the sea, backed by huge resources and the most modern weapons," said an incredulous Bobby Kennedy, younger brother of slain President John F. Kennedy, were being beaten by "an enemy whose total strength is about 250,000." Kennedy summed up the feelings of many Americans. Already Minnesota Senator Eugene McCarthy had entered the race for the Democratic nomination in the upcoming presidential election against Lyndon Johnson as a peace candidate. In March, McCarthy would stun Johnson by beating him in the New Hampshire primary. In the meantime, Bobby Kennedy's thoughts on critical national issues—civil rights, Vietnam, and the moral vacancy of a society of abundance— were leading him to believe that none of this would have happened if there had still been a Kennedy in the White House. In the same month that Kennedy entered the race for the presidency, Johnson withdrew. "I shall not seek, and I will not accept, the nomination of my party for another term as your president," Johnson announced on March 31, 1968.

While Johnson's failure and his withdrawal from the race were perhaps a triumph for the Anti-War Movement, the tragedies that were to come canceled any sense that good would come out of it. The same week as Johnson's announcement, Martin Luther King Jr. arrived in Memphis, Tennessee, to support sanitation workers who were on strike. One week later, King, America's greatest prophet of nonviolence, was assassinated on the balcony of the Lorraine Motel.

Over the next few days, the despair and sense of futility in the African-American community would erupt into flames across the country. In Washington, D.C., just a few blocks from the White House, and in Baltimore, Harlem, Atlanta, Chicago, and Kansas City, fires burned in the streets and 50,000 national and federal guardsmen rushed in to bring peace. More than one hundred cities were marked with violence, arson, looting, and gunfire. The indescribable grief was felt not only by blacks but by a whole country, that the man who stood for harmony in a divided nation could be taken from us so brutally.

The horror did not end with King's assassination. Two months later, after winning the California primary, Bobby Kennedy became the victim of an assassin's bullet. As the brother of a slain president, Bobby Kennedy had captured the imagination of the country. With the California win, he had been gaining momentum and had looked to be heading straight for the White House. Instead, he was brought down by a bullet. The nation seemed to be killing its heroes. Whatever bitterness Boomers were feeling began to seep into the rest of the country. A sense of the absurd began to dominate the culture.

- On television, *Rowan & Martin's Laugh-In* arrived to make fun of the establishment with fast cuts of irreverent humor spliced with a go-go dancer in body paint (Goldie Hawn).

*Poet Gary Snyder captured the sense of horror that many young people felt about the Vietnam War and started to feel about their own country, and even themselves. In this poem, Snyder celebrates all that is not white and middle class, in short, otherness.*

**A Curse on the Men in Washington, Pentagon**

As you shoot down the Vietnamese girls and men
    in their fields
Burning and chopping,
Poisoning and blighting,
So surely I hunt the white man down in my
      heart.
        The crew-cutted Seattle boy
          The Portland boy who worked for U.P.
           that was me.
           I won't let him live. The "American"
           I'll destroy. The "Christian" has long
           been dead.
           They won't pass on to my children.
           I'll give them Chief Joseph, the
            Bison herds,
         Ishi, sparrowhawk, the fir trees,
        The Buddha, their own naked bodies,
        Swimming and dancing and singing instead.
  As I kill the white man,
the "American" in me
And dance out the ghost dance:
To bring back America, the grass and the streams
To trample your throat in your dreams.
This magic I work, this loving I give
That my children may flourish
And yours won't live.

Half a million American soldiers with 700,000 Vietnamese allies...were being beaten by "an enemy whose total strength is about 250,000."

five buildings on the campus of Columbia University in New York City. The most notable of these uprisings, however, occurred in August at the Democratic National Convention in Chicago. The wind seemed to have been knocked out of the Democratic Party. It appeared it would never recover from the death of Bobby Kennedy and Martin Luther King Jr. McCarthy did not have the support of party insiders, and no one seemed to have the energy any longer to fight them. Hubert Humphrey, Johnson's vice president and the selection of the party bosses, appeared to have the nomination locked, bringing with him Johnson's policies and the status quo.

Watching these developments and feeling powerless to do anything about them, the radical youth felt driven over the edge. They reasoned that if the democratic process couldn't fix the country, then the only logical action was revolution.

- Rockers like Country Joe and the Fish began to sing ironically about Vietnam: "Be the first one on your block to have your boy come home in a box!"
- Simon and Garfunkel sang in a ballad "Where have you gone, Joe DiMaggio?" linking DiMaggio to a lost era where baseball and apple pie still meant something.
- The strange, the odd, and the absurd took hold of the nation's consciousness. One of the oddest manifestations was Tiny Tim, who sang '20s songs like "Tiptoe Through the Tulips" in a falsetto while playing the ukulele.

It was like the country had broken free of its moorings. In this anything-goes atmosphere, Boomers felt they had permission to seek their own personal happiness no matter what. In this same spring of '68, radicals seized

Martin Luther King Jr.: assassinated April 4, 1968. Race riots in over 100 cities.

Robert Kennedy: assassinated June 5, 1968.

ness, while outside the police were wreaking havoc on the protesters. The insane disconnect between what party bosses were orchestrating inside and the utter anarchy occurring outside was captured by television cameras and photographers. They documented both the boring speeches and the brutal violence that the police and the National Guard were committing on protesters. As the convention progressed each day, the horror grew. From outside Chicago, America appeared to be burning.

Jane Adams, born in 1943 and a member of SDS in 1968, described the experience on the streets:

**When Humphrey was nominated, I was in the YMCA watching it on TV. I ran out in the streets, and armored personnel carriers with barbed wires on the front of them moved into position. The young people chanted, "The whole world is watching," which really meant that the whole world is watching this massive injustice that's going on here, the ripping-off of our democracy from us.**

A protester described the scene:

**As soon as we got to Chicago there was a sense that this thing was going to be huge.... You couldn't help but be caught up in all the violence.... I remember standing in front of the Loop in a big demonstration when the cops came and pushed us through a plate-glass window, and there was glass all over and people were screaming, and their heads were bleeding.**

The protesters' bitterness and anger was emblematic and fueled the rage of 10,000 other protesters who descended on the Windy City. However, they were met with an even greater and heavily armed force—23,000 police and National Guardsmen. As anyone would expect, violence erupted almost immediately on the streets.

Inside the convention hall, politician after politician took the podium and droned on about American great-

Protesters began referring to Chicago during the Democratic National Convention as "Czechcago," making a comparison of the city's police to the brutal put-down of protesters in Prague that spring by 650,000 Soviet troops.

**The Chicago Seven and their lawyers at a press conference**

## THE CHICAGO SEVEN: A COURT CIRCUS

In an attempt to justify their extreme actions, the government indicted eight radical leaders for conspiring to incite riots. The eight leaders included David Dellinger, a pacifist and the chairman of the National Mobilization Committee to End the War in Vietnam; Tom Hayden and Rennie Davis, leaders of SDS; Abbie Hoffman and Jerry Rubin, leaders of the Youth International Party (YIP); John Froines and Lee Weiner, local Chicago organizers; and Bobby Seale, cofounder of the Black Panther Party.

Beginning in September, the trial was a circus. The prosecutors stressed the group's provocative rhetoric and subversive intentions. William Kunstler, the lawyer for all defendants—the Chicago Seven—except Seale, attributed the violence to overreaction by officials rather than a conspiracy. He paraded singers, artists, and activists to testify in court about what the demonstrators were protesting. During the trial, Weatherman (an SDS splinter group) proclaimed "Days of Rage" on the streets of Chicago.

Seale, however, refused to participate in the proceeding since his organization had not joined in the protests at the convention. When he became disruptive and hostile, the

judge ended up binding and gagging Seale for three days before declaring a mistrial and sentencing him to four years for contempt of court. The trial for the other seven lasted five months. They were found guilty in February 1970. Two years later, however, their convictions were overturned by an appeals court, which cited the judge's procedural errors and overt hostility toward the defendants. Sadly, Bobby Seale, the only African-American defendant who did not participate in the riots for which the eight were charged, was the only one who spent time in jail.

To add to the strangeness of the year, the Republicans nominated a man everyone thought was politically dead: Richard Milhous Nixon. Nixon had lost the 1960 presidential election to John F. Kennedy. His famous bitter words on that loss were: "You won't have Nixon to kick around anymore." Now Nixon was head of the Republican ticket, a man of proven experience, having been vice president for eight years during the Eisenhower Administration and a U.S. senator before that. Many had forgotten Nixon's nefarious past as one of the key supporters of the anti-Communist witch hunts of the early fifties. By

1968, he had been rehabilitated simply by the passing of time and the country's emotional reaction to the violence at the Democratic convention. As a symbol for calm and status quo, Nixon campaigned by talking about America's "silent majority," which he said still believed in the flag and the family, in the need to have a strong nation ready to fight Communism. In what seemed a spectacular failure of the youth movement, Nixon won the election and was sworn in as president in January 1969.

Nixon's presidency would drive many in the left even further into radical politics. The left had not forgotten Nixon's unethical behavior during McCarthyism and did not believe that he had changed. Instead they felt that they were being marginalized and that their freedom to express their beliefs was being threatened. Many imagined a return to the McCarthy hearings and the blacklisting of left-leaning citizens again. Though the country was in a much different place than in 1950 and the likelihood of something like that occurring again was remote, the radical left had reason to worry.

With Nixon's win, it was clear the radical left did not have broad support across the country. Leftists also would face an illegal and unethical attack from parts of the government, which helped to undermine what little support they did have. A secret task force called COINTELPRO (counterintelligence program) was formed by the FBI to carry out a plan to disrupt and destroy these radicals. By bugging offices, planting agents, and recruiting informers, the FBI manipulated public perception of these groups.

By 1969, many of the campus protest groups were becoming paranoid about information being leaked and were disintegrating into squabbling factions. The most notable radicalization was SDS, which splintered into the Progressive Labor Party and the Weatherman. Weatherman were notorious for their promotion of violence against the system. The group was literally blown apart on March 6, 1970, when a faulty pipe bomb destroyed a Manhattan town house, killing three members. The Progressive Labor

*Logically, or perhaps illogically when it comes to these two characters, Jerry Rubin and Abbie Hoffman took the lead in protesting the unfairness of the convention. They and the Yippies created a parallel mock agenda for the convention, called a "Festival of Life."*

## A STATEMENT FROM YIP

Join us in Chicago in August for an international festival of youth, music, and theater. Rise up and abandon the creeping meatball! Come all you rebels, youth spirits, rock minstrels, truthseekers, peacock-freaks, poets, barricadejumpers, dancers, lovers and artists!

It is summer. It is the last week in August, and the NATIONAL DEATH PARTY meets to bless Lyndon Johnson. We are there! There are 50,000 of us dancing in the streets, throbbing with amplifiers and harmony. We are making love in the parks. We are reading, singing, laughing, printing newspapers, groping, and making a mock convention, and celebrating the birth of FREE AMERICA in our own time.

Everything will be free. Bring blankets, tents, draft-cards, body-paint, Mrs. Leary's Cow, food to share, music, eager skin, and happiness. The threats of LBJ, Mayor Daley, and J. Edgar Freako will not stop us. We are coming! We are coming from all over the world!

The life of the American spirit is being torn asunder by the forces of violence, decay, and the napalm-cancer fiend. We demand the Politics of Ecstasy! We are the delicate spores of the new fierceness that will change America. We will create our own reality, we are Free America! And we will not accept the false theater of the Death Convention.

We will be in Chicago. Begin preparations now! Chicago is yours! Do it!

## THE DRAFT MYTH: WHO FOUGHT IN VIETNAM?

Approximately two thirds of the men who went to Vietnam enlisted and were not drafted. Most of these enlisted men came from working-class or poor families. On average, those who went to Vietnam were nineteen years old. In World War II, the average age was twenty-six.

For every young man drafted by the military in the '60s, seven were exempted by their draft boards. The Selective Service policy was "channeling manpower by deferment" into areas vital to national security. In reality, that meant that anyone who was in college received a deferment. Most teachers, engineers, scientists, and many other college-educated professionals received draft deferments. So did most "supervisors" of four or more workers as well as apprentice plumbers and electricians.

The group most creative in avoiding the draft were middle-class and upper-middle-class men. Once they had exhausted their deferments, they were able to find a variety of ingenious strategies to remain out of the military. Many used family connections to enter the National Guard and the Coast Guard. Others found sympathetic doctors or psychiatrists who vouched for their psychological instability or homosexuality. Some claimed to be members of subversive organizations such as the Communist Party. Some went to Canada, from where they could not be extradited back to the States. A half million young men became conscientious objectors and served by doing national service or nonfighting duties in the military. Both the first two Boomer Generation presidents avoided the draft. President Bill Clinton received a deferment, and President George W. Bush joined the Texas National Guard. Historians William Strauss and Lawrence Baskin cynically concluded that it was America's best and brightest who were able to avoid serving in the military. "The Vietnam draft cast the entire generation into a contest for individual survival...the 'fittest'—those with the background, wit, or money—managed to escape," Strauss and Baskin have written.

sect simply disappeared with a whimper.

Contributing to the demise of these groups' influence on the national debate about Vietnam and other issues was the growing inclusion of voices from more mainstream groups in the Anti-War Movement. These included, most notably, Vietnam Veterans Against the War (VVAW), Clergy and Laity Concerned About Vietnam, Another Mother for Peace, the Fellowship of Reconciliation, and the War Resisters League.

The groups were galvanized by the horrors that came both within the country and in Vietnam. On May 4, 1970, National Guardsmen opened fire on Kent State University students protesting President Nixon's expansion of the Vietnam War into neighboring Cambodia. Four students were killed, nine more wounded. Students on campuses across the nation were horrified and immediately called a strike, shutting down universities everywhere. These deaths seemed to announce an apocalyptic end to the era, but out of its ashes would arise a nation united against the war.

Historian Milton Viorst summed up the closing of the decade this way:

The decade ended because the Civil Rights Movement, which was responsible for its conception, no longer contributed to the seed to enrich it. It ended because antiwar protest, discredited at Chicago, never regained popular approval. It ended because a consensus was reached that the country had blundered in entering the war, and because Americans accepted the government's assurances that only time was needed until the last soldiers came home. The 1960s ended because a society can function at a feverish emotional pitch for only so long, and Americans, after ten years of it, were tired.

ALLISON B. KRAUSE

WILLIAM K. SCHROEDER

# "four dead in Ohio..."

—Crosby, Stills, Nash & Young, "Ohio"

JEFFREY G. MILLER

SANDRA L. SCHEUER

**Students killed at Kent State**

TURN OFF YOUR

RELAX AND FLOAT DOWN

IT IS NOT DYING, IT IS NOT

LAY DOWN ALL

SURRENDER TO THE

—"Tomorrow Never Knows," the Beatles

66

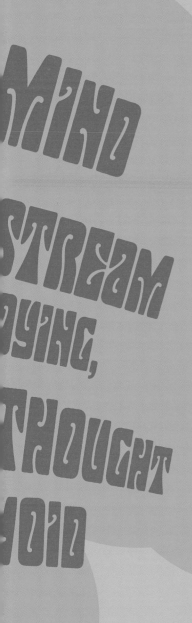

MIND STREAM DYING, THOUGHT VOID

# FEELING GROOVY

Just as the Beatles quickly moved past political radicalism, so did much of the Youth Movement. American youth was clearly against the Vietnam War, but their focus was on changing the culture, not fighting the political establishment.

# TURN ON

**HIPPIE**—a name originally coined by Beats to refer to young people who were trying to be hip, but weren't authentic Beats. Youths, however, quickly adopted "hippie" for members of the counterculture.

## PUSHING THE CONSUMER BOUNDARIES

"A minority of young people, bored with the legal drugs—tobacco, alcohol—and the other mass-market consumer items that were pushed at them on their TVs and radio with an energy and expertise that surpassed anything heard at school or in church, had begun to experiment with new products and new lifestyles. In pushing past the boundary of permissible consumer behavior they had begun breaking the law and frightening their parents."
—*Historian David Farber*

Hippie culture epitomized that spirit with its emphasis on freedom, self-expression, and pleasure. These long-haired youths agreed that the war was a "bad trip" and should be ended, but they would also admit that devoting themselves to protesting it was not their "bag." They were looking for something larger. They wanted to experience nirvana, a term they learned by reading about Eastern religions. Their route to this enlightened state was not always linear. Rather, it took an indirect route through experimentation with new experiences, such as listening to music, dropping acid, and smoking marijuana, as well as studying meditation, yoga, and other Eastern practices.

The Beatles seemed to internalize this spirit almost immediately. They quickly transitioned from their radical songs, which evoked the political resistance in the country, to a more psychedelic music. Songs like "Yellow Submarine," "Sergeant Pepper's Lonely Hearts Club Band," "Good Day Sunshine," and others contained an exotic, over-the-top, saturated sound that embodied the ecstatic energy of the youth. When their song "Tomorrow Never Knows" appeared on radio stations in 1966, it didn't sound like anything the Beatles had ever written and performed before, or anyone else for that matter. "In between what sounded like sallies by a vindictive flock of intergalactic crows, the lyrics—about turning off your mind and floating down an undying stream (unless the meaning was that turning off your mind was not the same as dying)—were actually quotations from Timothy Leary's *The Psychedelic Experience*," describes historian Charles Perry.

Boomer Alan Aldridge wrote, "I first became aware of the depth of the lyrics to the Beatles songs when I went to a party in 1967 during the Sergeant Pepper era. Someone whispered in my ear that 'Lucy in the Sky with Diamonds' was a song about an LSD trip."

And it was a "long strange trip," to quote one of the Grateful Dead's songs from the time. Dead drummer Bob Weir has said, "Not much of the ideology survived, but the music, the art, and the feeling behind it flourished."

# never trust anyone over 30!

Unlike the radicals who tried to change the system, hippies attempted, in the words of LSD guru Timothy Leary, to "tune in, drop out, and turn on." Leary and his counterparts, the Merry Pranksters, preached the amazing powers of the drug LSD to change one's consciousness and lead people into new levels of awareness. Until 1966 LSD was actually legal in the United States. With these proselytizers traveling the country extolling the wonders of LSD and other psychedelic drugs, a whole generation of young people became enamored with getting high. No one yet knew what a "bad trip" it would turn out to be.

Instead, getting high seemed like the perfect response to the pervading feeling of desolation. After the shock of Kennedy's assassination and the ever-present standoff with the Soviet Union that held the country on the brink of nuclear annihilation, young people were ready for any suggestion of a new way to feel good. The mass market had primed them for the next new thing, and here it was: LSD and other psychedelic drugs. These drugs promised to transform one's consciousness and bring anyone who "dropped a tab" to a new level of awareness.

## SUMMER OF LOVE

The epicenter of this new hippie culture was San Francisco's Haight-Ashbury district. It began in the spring of 1967 and lasted through the summer. America's youths left their homes and college dorms and made their way to San Francisco, where they were invited by the Haight-Ashbury council to a "Summer of Love," a months-long festival that became a media extravaganza.

The Council for the Summer of Love was founded by members of the Family Dog, the Diggers, the *Oracle* newspaper, the Straight Theater, and about twenty-five individuals. The Council was formed, according to their literature, "to serve as a central clearing house for theatrical, musical, and artistic events, dances, concerts and happenings in the Haight-Ashbury district." The Council also supported the Haight-Ashbury Free Clinic, the Huckleberry House for Runaways, the Diggers, and free concerts and happenings. In short, they acted as the unofficial host to more than 75,000 young people who trekked to the Haight during these summer months. These youths came to encounter a new way of experiencing the world, to discover new values to guide their lives, and to build a community of young people based on mutual respect and collaboration. With these high ideals, they felt they could create a utopia of their own. This also meant experimenting with something called "free love" and with drugs. The following is a list of the Haight hot spots.

Based on the song written by John Lennon and Paul McCartney, the movie *Yellow Submarine* revolves around the Beatles' adventure-filled journey to a peaceful kingdom of Pepperland, where, upon their arrival, they set out to save residents from an invasion by a group of "music-hating ogres" known as the Blue Meanies. Through their music and love, the foursome transform the Meanies into gentle creatures and restore happiness to Pepperland.

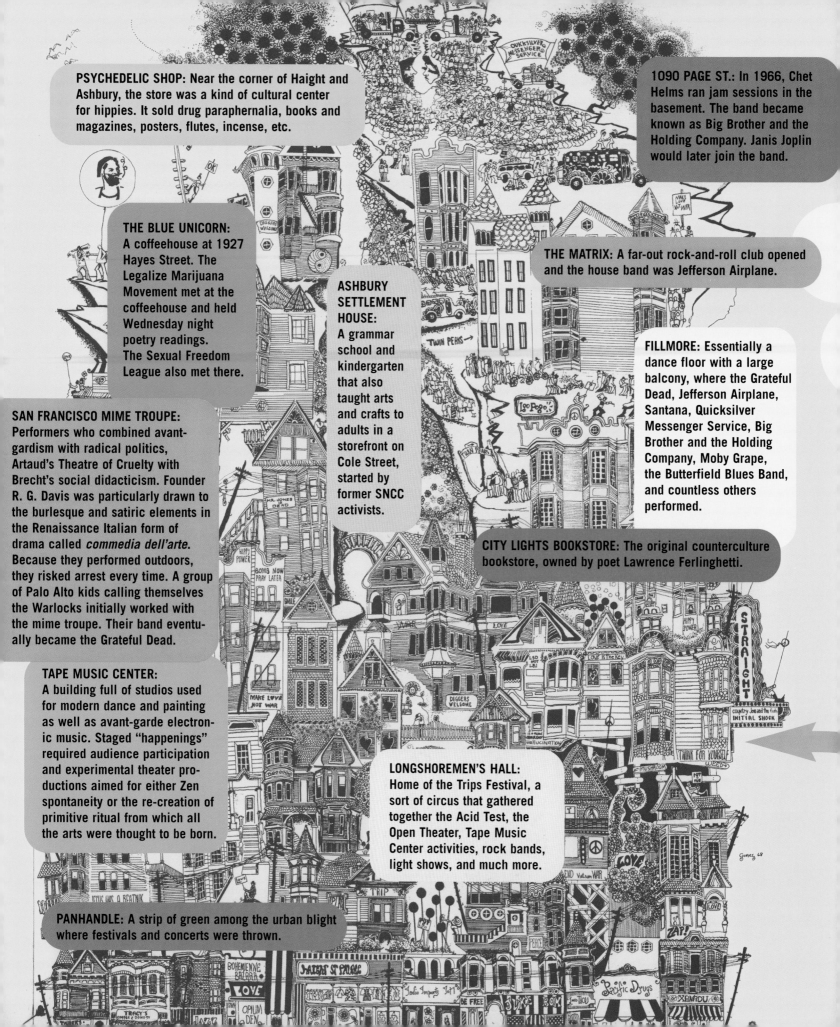

**PSYCHEDELIC SHOP:** Near the corner of Haight and Ashbury, the store was a kind of cultural center for hippies. It sold drug paraphernalia, books and magazines, posters, flutes, incense, etc.

**1090 PAGE ST.:** In 1966, Chet Helms ran jam sessions in the basement. The band became known as Big Brother and the Holding Company. Janis Joplin would later join the band.

**THE BLUE UNICORN:** A coffeehouse at 1927 Hayes Street. The Legalize Marijuana Movement met at the coffeehouse and held Wednesday night poetry readings. The Sexual Freedom League also met there.

**ASHBURY SETTLEMENT HOUSE:** A grammar school and kindergarten that also taught arts and crafts to adults in a storefront on Cole Street, started by former SNCC activists.

**THE MATRIX:** A far-out rock-and-roll club opened and the house band was Jefferson Airplane.

**SAN FRANCISCO MIME TROUPE:** Performers who combined avant-gardism with radical politics, Artaud's Theatre of Cruelty with Brecht's social didacticism. Founder R. G. Davis was particularly drawn to the burlesque and satiric elements in the Renaissance Italian form of drama called *commedia dell'arte*. Because they performed outdoors, they risked arrest every time. A group of Palo Alto kids calling themselves the Warlocks initially worked with the mime troupe. Their band eventually became the Grateful Dead.

**FILLMORE:** Essentially a dance floor with a large balcony, where the Grateful Dead, Jefferson Airplane, Santana, Quicksilver Messenger Service, Big Brother and the Holding Company, Moby Grape, the Butterfield Blues Band, and countless others performed.

**CITY LIGHTS BOOKSTORE:** The original counterculture bookstore, owned by poet Lawrence Ferlinghetti.

**TAPE MUSIC CENTER:** A building full of studios used for modern dance and painting as well as avant-garde electronic music. Staged "happenings" required audience participation and experimental theater productions aimed for either Zen spontaneity or the re-creation of primitive ritual from which all the arts were thought to be born.

**LONGSHOREMEN'S HALL:** Home of the Trips Festival, a sort of circus that gathered together the Acid Test, the Open Theater, Tape Music Center activities, rock bands, light shows, and much more.

**PANHANDLE:** A strip of green among the urban blight where festivals and concerts were thrown.

## COMMUNES:
## COUNTERCULTURE COMMUNITIES

These communities sprung up anywhere young people could congregate and begin a new way of life. They were called communes because they promoted communal living and the sharing of food and finances. The premise behind communes was to create a community where everyone was completely free to do as they pleased as long as they respected each other. This meant that there was a lot of experimentation in free love and drug use. Communes formed all over the country in apartment-houses, in cities, and in remote rural areas on farms. These places included:

Haight-Ashbury
Fourteenth Street in Atlanta
Old Town in Chicago
Lower East Side of New York City
Austin, Texas
Lawrence, Kansas
Fayetteville, Arkansas
Colfax Avenue in Denver

### CORNER OF HAIGHT AND MASONIC
Site of the Full Moon Public Celebration, organized by the Diggers and the San Francisco Mime Troupe. They brought a thirteen-foot-square wooden frame, painted yellow, that they called the Frame of Reference and encouraged people to step through it before being served at the daily free feeds.

The Diggers passed out seventy-five six-inch replicas of the Frame of Reference to be worn around the neck. They performed a playlet called "Any Fool on the Street" and then started the intersection game, which was a lesson in the Digger theory of ownership of the streets. Leaflets gave instructions to walk across the intersection in different directions to form various polygons, relying on the pedestrian's right of way over automobiles: "Don't wait don't walk (umbrella step, stroll, cake walk, somersault, finger-crawl, squat-jump, pilgrimage, Phylly dog, etc.)." It was a translation of the civil rights sit-in technique directed against automobiles, and at the same time a terrific goof.

## Media Frenzy

The Summer of Love was perhaps America's first media event. Scores of journalists, photographers, and television reporters descended on San Francisco. There were so many media people that a running joke started about bead-wearing *Life* magazine reporters interviewing bead-wearing *Look* magazine reporters because there were more of them than real hippies.

# THE DIGGERS

The Diggers were an anarchist group in San Francisco's Haight-Ashbury who wanted to break free of America's capitalistic system. Inspired by the English Diggers (1649–50), they tried to free the world from private property and all forms of buying and selling. Their goal was to create a Free City. They established a Free Store where everything was free for the taking and gave out Free Food every day in the park. The Diggers were at the center of many of the '60s iconic traditions. They were the first to proclaim the nutritious value of whole wheat bread over white bread with Free Digger Bread baked in one- and two-pound coffee cans. They established the first Free Medical Clinic. They started the tie-dyed clothing craze and communal celebrations of natural planetary events, such as the solstices and equinoxes.

A flyer handed out at Haight and the Panhandle by the Diggers:

FREE FOOD   GOOD HOT STEW
RIPE TOMATOES   FRESH FRUIT
BRING A BOWL AND A SPOON TO
THE PANHANDLE AT ASHBURY STREET
4PM  4PM  4PM  4PM
FREE FOOD   EVERDAY   FREE FOOD
IT'S FREE BECAUSE IT'S YOURS!
the diggers

## ENLIGHTENMENT FOR THE MASSES

In their quest for a better world and a better life, many young people found themselves gravitating toward non-Western religions and other new spiritual paths. Many made trips to India to study with gurus like the Maharishi Mahesh Yogi, who became the Beatles' spiritual adviser. In fact, the band announced in 1967 that they were giving up psychedelic drugs for meditation and went to India to study. Many celebrities followed, including actress Mia Farrow, Jets quarterback Joe Namath, architect Buckminster Fuller, and social critic Marshall McLuhan.

Others joined sects like the Hare Krishnas. Founded in 1965 in New York by A. C. Bhaktivedanta, a chemist and Sanskrit scholar from Calcutta, the International Society for Krishna Consciousness worshipped the Hindu deity Krishna. Bhaktivedanta's followers referred to him as Swami Prabhupada, shaved their heads, wore saffron robes, and devoted themselves to proselytizing. They became familiar figures in airports and on street corners, selling carnations and recruiting new members. Comic book artist R. Crumb satirized this impulse toward spiritual investigation in one of his early issues of *Zap Comix*.

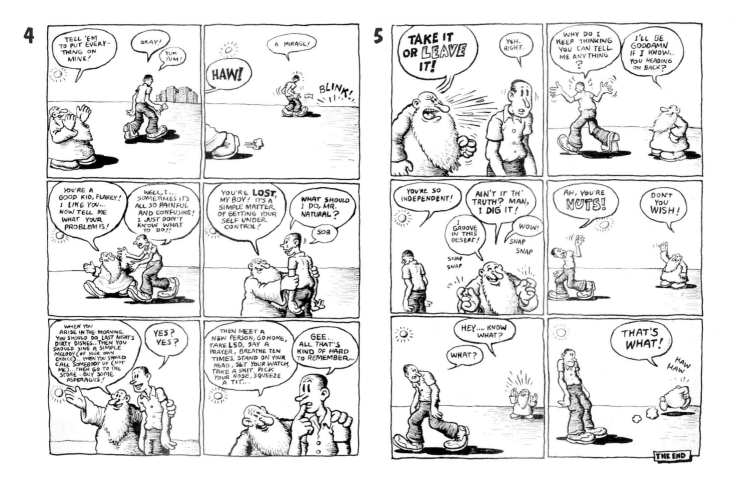

## ROBERT CRUMB

One day in 1966, Robert Crumb walked away from his job and impulsively accepted a ride to San Francisco. There, caught up in the burgeoning counterculture, he began using LSD. His drawing style and subject matter were permanently affected by the mind-altering drug. In 1967, he created *Zap Comix*, personally selling copies out of a baby carriage in the Haight-Ashbury district during the fabled "Summer of Love." The "underground" comic book became a cult hit, leading to two solo *Zap* sequels before Crumb characteristically began sharing the title's content and royalties with other Bay area artists. Though he did not regard himself as a "hippie," he nonetheless created such '60s and '70s icons as Mr. Natural, Flakey Foont, Fritz the Cat, Mr. Snoid, and the ubiquitous big-foot image "Keep-on-Truckin'."

# "Woodstock was not a concert. This was a coming together. What the Byrds called a Tribal Gathering. We came together in Bethel. Yes like Bethlehem, this was a meeting of the essence of the thing. The music was just the background music of our lives."

—Dr. Jan Pitts, who was at Woodstock

## WOODSTOCK NATION: AUGUST 15–17, 1969

Originally advertised as "three days of peace and music," Woodstock became the cultural touchstone for a generation. Trying to cash in on the wave of rock festivals that became popular in the late 1960s, Woodstock's promoters envisioned an event that would draw about 100,000 young people to hear performers including Jimi Hendrix, Joan Baez, Jefferson Airplane, Arlo Guthrie, and the Grateful Dead. Instead 500,000 people poured into 600 acres outside Bethel, New York, to become part of "Woodstock Nation." Amazingly, even with chronic food shortages, few bathrooms, inadequate medical facilities, no security, and heavy rain, the festival was relatively peaceful and convinced many participants and observers of the potential for creating alternative communities.

## ALTAMONT: NO MORE SHELTER

**War, children, it's just a shot away...**
**I tell you love, sister, it's just a kiss away...**

—The Rolling Stones' lyrics from "Gimme Shelter"

The Rolling Stones, responding to complaints about exorbitant concert ticket prices, agreed to perform a free concert in San Francisco at the end of their 1969 tour. The Grateful Dead, Santana, Jefferson Airplane, and Crosby, Stills, Nash, and Young also appeared. Poorly planned, the concert secured a venue, the Altamont Speedway, fewer than twenty-four hours before the event.

Three hundred thousand people showed up, many of them abandoning their cars on the highway and walking the last few miles to the racetrack. Concert "security" was provided by the Hell's Angels, many of them drunk or high on LSD. They proved particularly violent in beating fans back from the barely elevated stage. When the Rolling Stones finally came on, Hell's Angels surrounded them with their motorcycles. In an example of particularly poor judgment, when tension between the crowd and the Hell's Angels peaked, the Rolling Stones broke into the song "Sympathy for the Devil." The crowd surged and clashed with the Hell's Angels. An African-American man fleeing from the blows of the Angels pulled a gun. The Angels stabbed, beat, and kicked him to death. The concert film *Gimme Shelter* captured the event.

For many, the tragedy of Altamont signaled an end to the short-lived promise of the Summer of Love and the Woodstock Nation.

# BURN, BABY, BURN

## FED UP!

It took a bomb murdering four young girls in a church in Birmingham, Alabama.

It took the lynching of Emmett Till, a fourteen-year-old boy, along with thousands of lynchings over the previous seventy years.

It took the assassination of one of the nation's most respected civil rights leaders, Martin Luther King Jr.

It took the killing of three civil rights workers in Mississippi.

It took the gunning down of NAACP leader Medgar Evers.

It took tens of thousands of beatings, millions of humiliations and injustices.

**"The only time that nonviolence has been admired is when the Negroes practice it."**

—James Baldwin

# Blacks should be able to march safely in Mississippi without the protection of whites at their side.

**POWER TO THE PEOPLE**

Finally, after all these years of tragedy, young black Americans were confronting the limitations of nonviolence. They had been jailed, beaten, and shot too many times to accept the nonviolent credo that love alone could conquer hate. Passage of the 1964 Civil Rights Act did not stop racism and discrimination.

It wasn't until a sniper shot James Meredith, however, that the critical mass occurred to push young black people to reject their elders' nonviolent philosophy and begin to take action. In June of 1966, Meredith, the first black to enroll at the University of Mississippi, embarked on a "one-man pilgrimage against fear" from Memphis, Tennessee, to Jackson, Mississippi. When Meredith was wounded at the start by a gunshot fired by a white racist, civil rights leaders rushed to Memphis to rescue Meredith's pilgrimage.

Quickly, leaders of mainstream organizations, such as the NAACP, the National Urban League, and the SCLC, clashed with young members of the more militant CORE and SNCC. At issue was the mainstream organizations' integrationist approach. CORE and SNCC leaders reasoned that blacks should be able to march safely in Mississippi without the protection of whites at their side. It was their civil right, and no one was going to dilute it or stop them from exercising that right. A militant black defense group, called Deacons for Defense and Justice, was formed to protect marchers. These Deacons armed themselves with guns.

Most of the civil rights establishment was offended by these actions and withdrew from Memphis. The exception was Martin Luther King Jr. and the SCLC, who participated reluctantly. Within days of Meredith's wounding, the march resumed but with a decidedly militant aura.

When the marchers reached Greenwood, Mississippi, newly elected SNCC president Stokely Carmichael led chants of "Black Power! Black Power!" In this cry there was no sense of accommodation. For these young firebrands, it was a battle cry for a new era in black rights. Black Power!

The Black Power Movement didn't come into existence out of thin air. It had several important precursors. The earliest was perhaps Marcus Garvey, who in the '20s preached black pride and a separatist back-to-Africa message. Garvey declared in a speech at the time:

whites; they simply were not concerned about how whites perceived them and instead focused on their people. Their mission was to uplift the race, not make whites feel better about blacks. One important aspect of this mission was pride and respect. The uniforms, parades, and titles were effective tools in achieving these goals.

> The time has come for the Negro to forget and cast behind him his hero worship and adoration of the other races, and to start out immediately to create and emulate **heroes of his own**. We must canonize our own martyrs, and elevate to positions of fame and honor black men and women who have made their distinct contributions to our racial history.

Garvey galvanized primarily working-class African Americans in a program of self-help and African nationalism. He created the Universal Negro Improvement Association (UNIA). At its height, UNIA had an estimated 6 million members, published the largest black weekly newspaper—*Negro World*—created a myriad of black self-help institutions, and ran numerous businesses. However, in his efforts to nurture black pride, he also attracted the ire of many middle-class educated blacks. Ever-conscious of how the white world viewed them, they were offended by UNIA's extravagant uniforms and the elaborate titles awarded its members, which to them seemed suggestive of minstrel shows.

Garvey and his followers weren't necessarily hostile to

Like the Black Power Movement that would come decades later, UNIA was not interested in accommodation or integration. Garvey and his followers believed that blacks deserved and needed a separate, nonwhite nation in which blacks would be the majority. Their answer was to return to Africa. Because of mismanagement and attacks by outsiders—both white and black—this vision was never achieved. Nevertheless, UNIA's aspirations and influence continue to this day.

After the fall of Garvey and UNIA, the 1930s saw another black nationalist movement that was much more successful. The Lost-Found Nation of Islam, or Black Muslims, was founded by a door-to-door silk salesman named Wali Farad Muhammad (born Wallace Fard). Farad's new religious organization veered from traditional Islam significantly. In particular, Black Muslims did not stress fulfillment of the

**Marcus Garvey**

"five pillars" of Islam. Much like UNIA, they were more interested in uplifting the race and nurturing black pride. Farad did this by constructing liturgy based not so much on historical facts as on a desire of what the truth ought to be. His vision for the Nation of Islam (the "Lost-Found" was eventually dropped) encompassed a mythology that explained the historical oppression of black people. In this doctrine, black people were originally members of the Shabazz tribe, which was the original race of humans and came to earth 66 trillion years ago. Farad went on to explain that white people were the result of an experiment performed by the evil scientist Yakub 6,000 years ago. Though this myth might seem outrageous today, it provided a framework for many new adherents to the Nation of Islam on which to base their sense of pride and self-esteem.

Almost immediately, Farad found a promising student, Elijah Muhammad (born Elijah Poole in Sandersville, Georgia). After three years of study, Elijah Muhammad established a temple in Chicago. Shortly after, Farad disappeared without a trace, leaving 8,000 adherents in Detroit. Muhammad assumed leadership of the fledgling Nation of Islam and quickly expanded its membership by emphasizing practical strategies for improving the lives of black people in the United States. The Nation of Islam's strident advocacy attracted many black Americans, particularly a young man in prison for burglary, Malcolm Little. While in prison, Little changed his name to Malcolm X in order to repudiate the name given to his family by white slaveholders, a practice that would be adopted by many other Black Muslims. In 1952, Malcolm X began

**Nation of Islam leader Elijah Muhammad.**

preaching at Temple 11 in Boston and quickly became the Honorable Elijah Muhammad's protégé.

A brilliant and inspired speaker, Malcolm X drew large crowds with his message of black nationalism. His speeches were mesmerizing and quotable. When speaking about the fight for civil rights, he argued that it had to be achieved "by any means necessary," not just through nonviolent means. He believed that eventually the country would have to resort to violence. Whites would not stop discriminating unless forced to. He said, "I believe that there will ultimately be a clash between the oppressed and those that do the oppressing. I believe that there will be a clash between those who want freedom, justice, and equality for everyone and those who want to continue the systems of exploitation." In the article "Racism: The Cancer That Is Destroying America," Malcolm X explained the reasoning behind his conclusions:

The common goal of 22 million Afro-Americans is respect as human beings, the God-given right to be a human being. Our common goal is to obtain the human rights that America has been denying us. We can never get civil rights in America until our human rights are first restored. We will never be recognized as citizens there until we are first recognized as humans.

Malcolm X was assassinated a year before the Black Power Movement emerged, but he was both an inspiration and an icon for those who followed.

The last of the influences on the Black Power Movement was the rise of Pan-Africanism in the '50s and '60s. This movement had goals similar to UNIA's and the

"We will never be recognized as citizens . . . until we are first recognized as humans."

—Malcolm X

**"Integration is a subterfuge** for the maintenance of white supremacy and reinforces, among both black and white, the idea that 'white' is automatically better and 'black' is by definition inferior."

—Stokely Carmichael in September 1966

Nation of Islam's, but its focus was the Third World, where blacks lived under white colonial rule. Pan-Africanism had three primary goals:

1. Search for black identity.
2. Struggle against colonialism.
3. Establish free nations governed by their people.

Dr. Frantz Fanon, the leading intellectual of the movement, made an argument for rebelling against white colonial power that went beyond Malcolm X's case for inevitability. In his examination of the destruction of colonialism, *The Wretched of the Earth*, Fanon wrote:

> The practice of violence binds [colonized people] together as a whole, since each individual forms a violent link in a great chain, a part of the great organism of violence which has surged upward in reaction to the settler's violence in the beginning.... It introduces into each man's consciousness the idea of a common cause, of a national destiny, and of a collective history.

In this passage Fanon makes the point that violence does not simply fight against oppression but also unites the oppressed in their efforts to cast off their tormenters. As a result, violence is an essential part of the search for identity. Without it, blacks would not find themselves. In psychological terms, blacks could understand themselves only in opposition to whites. That is why people of African origin call themselves black; they are the opposite of white.

These movements—their actions and justifications—would resonate with young black Americans and guide them in the creation of the Black Power Movement in the later half of the '60s.

## THE ANATOMY OF A RIOT

"Burn! Baby, Burn!" rose the cry of an angry mob on August 12, 1965, on the streets of the Watts section of Los Angeles. And thousands of African Americans were doing just that to their homes, to their businesses, to their streets.

The day before, a young black man was pulled over for a routine traffic violation. The young man behind the wheel was drunk and verbally abusive toward the police officers who had pulled over the car. His disturbance quickly drew an audience on the crowded street. In Watts, a young black man in a confrontation with white police officers was not unusual. Of the 205 police officers in the 98 percent black L.A. ghetto, 200 were white. As the crowd watched the officers pull the young man from the car, they witnessed something that seemed all too common: white police officers manhandling a black man. When the young man's brother became abusive toward the officers, they manhandled him roughly as well.

For some reason on this hot August day, this aggressive arrest was simply one too many. The crowd quickly became a mob. Rocks and bottles showered down upon the police officers. More officers were called in, and the confrontation escalated from a simple arrest into a community at war. By the next morning, the neighborhood had begun destroying itself. Fires were set. Stores were looted. White drivers were attacked. For five days, the streets were filled with violence and rage. More than 15,000 police and National Guardsmen descended on the community, which only seemed to intensify the fury.

By August 16, thirty people had been killed, more than 1,000 injured, and 4,000 arrested. Property damage was estimated at between $35 and $45 million, a number almost beyond conception in this poor neighborhood.

America was stunned. The myth in white America had been that race problems were limited to the South and that those problems were being addressed in legislation such as the 1964 Civil Rights Act, the War on Poverty in 1965, and the Voting Rights Act, signed just days earlier on August 6. That black people in Los Angeles, the so-called city of angels and endless summer, were willing not simply to riot but to destroy their own community, was a shock.

What would drive someone to burn their own home?

### RIOT IN THE STREETS

Watts was the first major riot of the 1960s. In the next three years, hundreds would follow, including in Newark, Detroit, Washington, D.C., Philadelphia, and Cleveland. Many of the most violent riots during these years were sparked by a single police incident. Police forces across the country were predominantly white and saw themselves as the only barrier between order and chaos. They viewed their work in the ghettos of America's cities as a war in "the jungle." For them this justified the use of excessive force with whatever was necessary and available—hands, feet, batons, and guns—to maintain order.

CORE worker Lou Smith assessed the causes behind the Watts riot:

> What happened was that people had sat there and watched all the concern about black people "over there." And there wasn't a damn soul paying one bit of attention to what was going on in Watts. So the black people in Watts just spontaneously rose up one day and said, Fuck it! We're hungry. Our schools stink. We're getting the shit beat out of us. **We tried the integration route. It's obvious the integration route isn't going to work. Now we've got to go another way.**

When a gang of youth spotted Martin Luther King Jr. on a visit to Watts afterward, they crowed, "We won!" King asked them how they could call death, destruction, and the alienation of white support winning. One young teen replied:

**We won because we made them pay attention to us.**

Indeed they did. A riot of such violence seemed inconceivable to those who were reaping the benefits of America's booming economy. What white America did not understand was the overwhelming despair that people who lived in ghettos like Watts felt. The unemployment rate in Watts was 30 percent. Los Angeles is a sprawling city with inadequate public transportation; if a person could not afford a car, he could not get to a job. Forty percent of Watts residents did not own a car.

At the same time, the housing was inadequate and horribly overpriced. Even middle-class blacks were locked into the ghetto because white communities restricted blacks. The consequences of housing stress was higher rents for worse housing in densely packed areas. To compound the problem, banks and savings and loans refused to approve mortgages in black neighborhoods on the reasoning that they were too crowded and unstable to be good investments. Without money available to invest in purchasing homes and improving the housing stock, landlords had no incentive to maintain and improve their properties. They knew they could rent them no matter how substandard. Ironically, housing segregation was worse outside of the South. With the focus always so heavily on the outrageousness of white Southern racists, these truths about Northern racism gained little attention.

**police brutality**
**segregation**
**unskilled workforce**
**bad schools**
**no mortgage**
**ghetto housing**
**30% unemployment**
**no car no job**
**no public transportation**
**LOS ANGELES**

further and further out of reach.

Lastly, and perhaps most importantly, rising expectations generated increased frustration. With the mass media, politicians, and many African-American leaders proclaiming a new era of possibility, people came to expect their situation to improve. Nineteenth-century French critic Alexis de Tocqueville wrote, "Evils which are patiently endured when they seem inevitable become intolerable when once the idea of escape from them is suggested." Escape *had* been suggested. The possibility that conditions would change offered hope. The rate at which these changes were being made was slow, and inspired anger and frustration—emotions capable of igniting violence.

That cry of "We won!" after the Watts riots defined the sense of triumph by many blacks. The fear that such violence instilled in whites was intoxicating for a people who lived their lives with a sense of powerlessness. It was one of the few opportunities to feel powerful, especially against their oppressors. It was as if these uneducated, unskilled youths had taken a page right out of Frantz Fanon's *The Wretched of the Earth* as they began to redefine their relationship with their oppressor. One young rioter confirms this:

I felt invincible.... Honestly, that was how powerful I felt. I'm not too proud of what I did, looking back. But I held nothing back. I let out all my frustration with every brick, every bottle that I threw.... Many people ran around looting the stores.... My only thought about the stores was something like, "Those store owners will be furious, but who cares. They aren't black. They don't know what furious really is." Then I picked up a bottle and tried to destroy a TV in the window display. I remember feeling completely relieved. I unleashed all the emotions that had built up inside, ones I didn't know how to express.

In addition to unemployment and substandard housing, the schools in these communities did not provide adequate education. As a result, two thirds of all adults in Watts lacked a high school diploma, and nearly two thirds of Watts high school students failed to graduate. With this kind of education failure widespread, it became a self-perpetuating cycle. Parents were qualified only for unskilled, low-paying jobs and were unprepared to help lift their children, through educational enrichment at home, to better opportunities.

Unlike uneducated, unskilled immigrants who'd settled in urban areas in the first half of the twentieth century, blacks moving out of the South after World War II found a work environment that had changed dramatically. In the past, urban migrants used unskilled jobs as the first step to a better life. Now, with advancing technology, these jobs were quickly becoming in short supply and

BLACK PANTHERS

# "The Revolution has co-ome, it's time to pick up the gu-un. Off the pigs!"

An intimidating group of young black men, dressed in black berets and leather jackets, marched in military formation through the streets of Oakland, California, chanting: "The Revolution has co-ome, it's time to pick up the gu-un. Off the pigs!"

The Black Panther Party for Self-Defense was the brainchild of two African-American activists, Bobby Seale and Huey Newton, and was formed in October 1966. Created to embody Malcolm X's doctrine of community self-defense, the party argued that the black community needed to arm itself in order to protect it from the white racist police. They were responding not only to the riots in Watts but also to the shooting of a fifteen-year-old boy by an off-duty police lieutenant in Harlem in 1964 and the killing of a fifteen-year-old youth shot in the back by a police officer in San Francisco in 1966. Increasingly, black neighborhoods felt more threatened than protected by police.

More and more activists were influenced by Frantz Fanon, whose works analyzed the destructive nature of colonial systems and provided an intellectual basis for revolutionary movements overseas. What dawned on these African-American readers was just how similar their circumstances were to colonies in Africa. Urban African-American communities were governed by a white power structure, where often the only whites that black people encountered were aggressive and hostile police.

The Black Panthers' initial mission was to monitor the police and defend themselves by carrying guns, which under California law was legal if the weapons were unconcealed. They drafted a ten-point program, modeled after the Declaration of Independence, to explain their party's platform.

## THE TEN-POINT PLAN

1. WE WANT FREEDOM. WE WANT POWER TO DETERMINE THE DESTINY OF OUR BLACK AND OPPRESSED COMMUNITIES.
We believe that Black and oppressed people will not be free until we are able to determine our destinies in our own communities ourselves, by fully controlling all the institutions which exist in our communities.

2. WE WANT FULL EMPLOYMENT FOR OUR PEOPLE.
We believe that the federal government is responsible and obligated to give every person employment or a guaranteed income. We believe that if the American businessmen will not give full employment, then the technology and means of production should be taken from the businessmen and placed in the community so that the people of the community can organize and employ all of its people and give a high standard of living.

3. WE WANT AN END TO THE ROBBERY BY THE CAPITALISTS OF OUR BLACK AND OPPRESSED COMMUNITIES.
We believe that this racist government has robbed us and now we are demanding the overdue debt of forty acres and two mules. Forty acres and two mules were promised 100 years ago as restitution for slave labor and the mass murder of Black people. We will accept the payment in currency which will be distributed to our many communities. The American racist has taken part in the slaughter of our fifty million Black people. Therefore, we feel this is a modest demand that we make.

4. WE WANT DECENT HOUSING, FIT FOR THE SHELTER OF HUMAN BEINGS.
We believe that if the landlords will not give decent housing to our Black and oppressed communities, then housing and the land should be made into cooperatives so that the people in our communities, with government aid, can build and make decent housing for the people.

5. WE WANT DECENT EDUCATION FOR OUR PEOPLE THAT EXPOSES THE TRUE NATURE OF THIS DECADENT AMERICAN SOCIETY. WE WANT EDUCATION THAT TEACHES US OUR TRUE HISTORY AND OUR ROLE IN THE PRESENT-DAY SOCIETY.
We believe in an educational system that will give to our people a knowledge of the self. If you do not have knowledge of yourself and your position in the society and in the world, then you will have little chance to know anything else.

6. WE WANT COMPLETELY FREE HEALTH CARE FOR ALL BLACK AND OPPRESSED PEOPLE.

We believe that the government must provide, free of charge, for the people, health facilities which will not only treat our illnesses, most of which have come about as a result of our oppression, but which will also develop preventive medical programs to guarantee our future survival. We believe that mass health education and research programs must be developed to give all Black and oppressed people access to advanced scientific and medical information, so we may provide ourselves with proper medical attention and care.

7. WE WANT AN IMMEDIATE END TO POLICE BRUTALITY AND MURDER OF BLACK PEOPLE, OTHER PEOPLE OF COLOR, ALL OPPRESSED PEOPLE INSIDE THE UNITED STATES.

We believe that the racist and fascist government of the United States uses its domestic enforcement agencies to carry out its program of oppression against Black people, other people of color and poor people inside the United States. We believe it is our right, therefore, to defend ourselves against such armed forces and that all Black and oppressed people should be armed for self-defense of our homes and communities against these fascist police forces.

8. WE WANT AN IMMEDIATE END TO ALL WARS OF AGGRESSION.

We believe that the various conflicts which exist around the world stem directly from the aggressive desire of the United States ruling circle and government to force its domination upon the oppressed people of the world. We believe that if the United States government or its lackeys do not cease these aggressive wars it is the right of the people to defend themselves by any means necessary against their aggressors.

9. WE WANT FREEDOM FOR ALL BLACK AND OPPRESSED PEOPLE NOW HELD IN U.S. FEDERAL, STATE, COUNTY, CITY AND MILITARY PRISONS AND JAILS. WE WANT TRIALS BY A JURY OF PEERS FOR ALL PERSONS CHARGED WITH SO-CALLED CRIMES UNDER THE LAWS OF THIS COUNTRY.

We believe that the many Black and poor oppressed people now held in United States prisons and jails have not received fair and impartial trials under a racist and fascist judicial system and should be free from incarceration. We believe in the ultimate elimination of all wretched, inhuman penal institutions, because the masses of men and women imprisoned inside the United States or by the United States military are the victims of oppressive conditions which are the real cause of their imprisonment. We believe that when persons are brought to trial they must be guaranteed, by the United States, juries of their peers, attorneys of their choice and freedom from imprisonment while awaiting trial.

10. WE WANT LAND, BREAD, HOUSING, EDUCATION, CLOTHING, JUSTICE, PEACE AND PEOPLE'S COMMUNITY CONTROL OF MODERN TECHNOLOGY.

When, in the course of human events, it becomes necessary for one people to dissolve the political bonds which have connected them with another, and to assume, among the powers of the earth, the separate and equal station to which the laws of nature and nature's God entitle them, a decent respect to the opinions of mankind requires that they should declare the causes which impel them to the separation.

We hold these truths to be self-evident, that all men are created equal; that they are endowed by their Creator with certain unalienable rights; that among these are life, liberty, and the pursuit of happiness. That to secure these rights, governments are instituted among men, deriving their just powers from the consent of the governed; that, whenever any form of government becomes destructive of these ends, it is the right of the people to alter or to abolish it, and to institute a new government, laying its foundation on such principles, and organizing its powers in such form as to them shall seem most likely to effect their safety and happiness. Prudence, indeed, will dictate that governments long established should not be changed for light and transient causes; and, accordingly, all experience hath shown that mankind are most disposed to suffer, while evils are sufferable, than to right themselves by abolishing the forms to which they are accustomed. But, when a long train of abuses and usurpation, pursuing invariably the same object, evinces a design to reduce them under absolute despotism, it is their right, it is their duty, to throw off such government, and to provide new guards for their future security.

At its height, the Black Panther Party had chapters in twenty-five cities including New York, Los Angeles, Detroit, Oakland, Des Moines, and Jersey City.

Regardless of the eloquence or reasonableness of most of these claims, the Black Panthers took such an intimidating approach to black justice that they were quickly villainized in the white media. The FBI director J. Edgar Hoover described the Panthers as "hoodlum-type revolutionaries." Even though the Panthers provided many social services in black communities, including free breakfast programs, welfare counseling, free medical clinics and other social services in several cities, their insistence on heated rhetoric ("offing the pigs"), carrying guns, and donning military attire overshadowed any good they were doing.

A confrontation between the Panthers and the police was inevitable. In October 1967, Panther leader Huey Newton went to jail for killing a police officer. In April of the following year, thirteen Panthers ambushed an Oakland police car, hitting it with 157 shots and badly wounding the officer. By 1970, the Panthers had killed eleven police officers. With each confrontation, the Panthers drew more recruits. Many of these recruits, however, were ex-convicts who had a beef against the police and delighted in being at war with America. As time passed, the Panthers seemed to devolve into a criminal organization. The party platform became a front to rip off and terrorize their own black neighbors.

### BLACK IS BEAUTIFUL

We want "poems that kill."
Assassin poems, Poems that shoot
guns. Poems that wrestle cops into alleys
and take their weapons leaving them dead....

We want a black poem. And a
Black World.
Let the world be a Black Poem
And Let All Black People Speak This Poem
Silently
or LOUD

—"Black Art," Imamu Amiri Baraka (LeRoi Jones)

With this poem, Baraka, who at the time still called himself LeRoi Jones, was inspired by the same sense of frustration that many young black Americans were feeling. Like other black radicals, he resented the real gap between what the law said was their rights and what rights they could actually demand. Because of this discrepancy, he and many other African-American artists and intellectuals set out to create a new role for themselves that was perhaps more political than aesthetic. They wanted their art to change American society and called their group the Black Arts Movement. In order to do this, they felt they had to transform African-American culture from one of subjugation to one of pride and celebration. In his manifesto for the movement, Baraka wrote:

### State/meant

The Black Artist's role in America is to aid in the destruction of America as he knows it. His role is to report and reflect so precisely the nature of the society, and of himself in that society, that other men will be moved by the exactness of his rendering and, if they are black men, grow strong through this moving, having seen their own strength, and weakness; and if they are white men, tremble, curse, and go mad, because they will be drenched with the filth of their evil.

The Black Artist must draw out of his soul the correct image of the world. He must use this image to band his brothers and sisters together in common understanding of the nature of the world (and the nature of America) and the nature of the human soul.

The Black Artist must demonstrate sweet life, how it differs from the deathly grip of the White Eyes. The Black Artist must teach the White Eyes their deaths, and teach the black man how to bring these deaths about.

**Imamu Amiri Baraka**

We are unfair, and unfair.
We are black magicians, black art
s we make in black labs of the heart.

The fair are
fair, and death
ly white.

The day will not save them
and we own
the night.

# BLACK IS

"If we had not had a Black Arts Movement in the sixties we certainly wouldn't have had national Black literary figures like Henry Louis Gates, Jr., Alice Walker, or Toni Morrison, because much more so than the Harlem Renaissance, in which Black artists were always on the leash of white patrons and publishing houses, **the Black Arts Movement did it for itself.** What you had was Black people going out nationally, in mass, saying that we are an independent Black people and this is what we produce."

—Robert Chrisman, founder with
Nathan Hare of *Black Scholar* in 1969

## BLACK ARTS ORGANIZATIONS

**New York City – BARTS**

**Detroit – Black Arts Midwest, Concept East**

**New Orleans – BLKARTSOUTH, Free Southern Theatre**

**Miami – Theatre of Afro Arts**

**Houston – Sudan Arts Southwest**

**San Francisco – Black Arts West**

**Newark, NJ – Spirit House**

**Chicago – The Organization of Black American Culture, Kuumba Theatre Company**

**Los Angeles – Ebony Showcase, Inner City Repertory Company, Performing Arts Society of Los Angeles**

In March of 1965, following the February assassination of Malcolm X, Baraka moved from the Lower East Side of Manhattan uptown to Harlem. This move was more than just a physical move. It was also a psychological move for Baraka and the other artists who joined him. Baraka and the others, including Askia Touré and Larry Neal, were shedding their integrationist position. Baraka was a celebrated poet, music critic, OBIE Award–winning playwright, and a major figure in the white literary establishment. He rejected that position and moved into a brownstone on 130th Street near Lenox Avenue, where he founded the Black Arts Repertory Theatre/School (BARTS). "The announcement of our arrival in Harlem was a parade, with the small group of young Black artists, led by the great genius Sun Ra and his then Myth Science Arkestra," wrote Baraka years later. For eight weeks that summer, BARTS led a festival of the Black Arts in the streets of Harlem. Using five trucks and folding tables as stages, they brought poetry, drama, painting, music, and dance every night to playgrounds, street corners, vacant lots, and parks. Their mission was to celebrate the new idea of "Blackness" as a liberating force.

BARTS, however, was much too revolutionary even for many blacks. It promoted violence and the overthrow of the government as the ways to achieve their goals. Obviously, this kind of extremism could not sustain itself. Nevertheless, the ambitions of this group and others less radical would eventually change American culture.

# BEAUTIFUL

In later years, Baraka wrote about what the Black Arts Movement was really about:

> To fight in the super structure, in the realm of ideas, philosophies, the arts, academia, the class struggle between the oppressed and the oppressor. To re-create and maintain our voice as a truly self-conscious, self-determining entity, to interpret and focus our whole lives and history. And create those organizations and institutions that will finally educate, employ, entertain, and liberate us!

Others also participated in making these goals a reality. Around the same time that BARTS was being organized, Dr. Robert Pritchard helped establish a guild society called the American Festival of Negro Art, which promoted Africa as the "fount and reservoir of our cultural strength." In Sumter, South Carolina, Morris College sponsored Negro History Week, which featured African arts and crafts, a special course on the Swahili language, and presentations on black history in the United States and black contributions to American culture through jazz and literature. It seemed like every black community was coming alive with festivals celebrating blackness. These efforts quickly helped African Americans redefine themselves within society by emphasizing their African and Caribbean heritage.

## REJECTING "NEGRO"

Young blacks were offended by the term "Negro," because it was an identity chosen by whites. They began looking for a name that blacks constructed themselves and that reflected the black community. The first choice was "Black." As the discussion evolved in the '60s and beyond, a more ethnic reference emerged: Afro American. This then evolved into African American because it encouraged the community to value its own heritage.

The late '60s and early '70s became the "Black Is Beautiful" era. Symbols of African heritage became prevalent everywhere: new "Afro" haircuts, dashiki shirts, African robes. West Coast nationalist Maulana Ron Karenga developed a black cultural catechism, which included a black holiday (Kwanzaa), the Swahili language, and cultural imagery of traditional Tanzanian society.

What began with black militants attempting to create a heightened sense of group identity quickly turned into a deeper and more accurate understanding of black people. This challenged traditional Eurocentric norms that for more than three centuries of slavery and segregation had forced blacks into an inferior role. It also opened the doors for other non-European cultures to finally take their rightful place in the American mosaic.

# WOMEN
# WORKING

# OUR BODIES

## WOMEN TAKING CONTROL OF THEIR DESTINY

### THE PROBLEM WITH NO NAME

The problem lay buried, unspoken, for many years in the minds of American women. It was a strange stirring, a sense of dissatisfaction, a yearning that women suffered in the middle of the twentieth century in the United States. Each suburban wife struggled with it alone. As she made the beds, shopped for groceries, matched slipcover material, ate peanut butter sandwiches with her children, chauffeured Cub Scouts and Brownies, lay beside her husband at night—she was afraid to ask even of herself the silent question—

### "Is this all?"

# OUR POLITICS

# Just what was this problem that has no name?

This excerpt from Betty Friedan's 1963 groundbreaking book, *The Feminine Mystique*, describes the dissatisfaction felt by women all across the country. Its publication was an event that redefined American culture and put words to the feelings that many women were having—the problem that had no name.

## I feel as if I don't exist.

Friedan stumbled upon her topic at her fifteen-year college reunion at Smith, a women's college. A housewife and freelance magazine writer, she crafted a questionnaire for her two hundred fellow classmates to fill out. The results confirmed something that she had been feeling herself—most of these highly educated, middle-class women were unhappy and did not know why.

Just what was this problem that has no name? What were the words women used when they tried to express it? Sometimes a woman would say "I feel empty somehow . . . incomplete." Or she would say, "I feel as if I don't exist." Sometimes she blotted out the feeling with a tranquilizer. Sometimes she thought the problem was with her husband or her children, or that what she really needed was to redecorate her house, or move to a better neighborhood, or have an affair, or another baby. Sometimes she went to a doctor with symptoms she could hardly describe: "A tired feeling . . . I get so angry with the children it scares me. . . . I feel like crying without any reason." (A Cleveland doctor called it "the housewife's syndrome.") A number of women told me about great bleeding blisters that break out on their hands and arms. "I call it the housewife's blight" said a family doctor in Pennsylvania. "I see it so often lately in these young women with four, five and six children who bury themselves in their dishpans. But it isn't caused by detergent and it isn't cured by cortisone."

The irony of her discovery was that no one initially wanted to hear what she had to say. Her research contradicted all the traditional assumptions about femininity—"a woman's place was in the home." She was turned down by three women's magazines because, according to them, the topic was not pertinent to women.

Eventually, the book sparked a national debate about a woman's role in society and in time was recognized as one of the central works of the modern Women's Movement.

## The women who suffer this problem have a hunger that food cannot fill.

It is NO longer possible to ignore that voice, to dismiss the desperation of so many American women. This is not what being a woman means, no matter what the experts say. For human suffering there is a reason; perhaps the reason has not been found because the right questions have not been asked, or pressed far enough. I do not accept the answer that there is no problem because American women have luxuries that women in other times and lands never dreamed of; part of the strange newness of the problem is that it cannot be understood in terms of the age-old material problems of man: poverty, sickness, hunger, cold. The women who suffer this problem have a hunger that food cannot fill. . . . It is not caused by lack of material advantages; it may not even be

## I feel empty somehow . . . incomplete.

Betty Friedan

We can no longer ignore that voice within women that says: "I want something more than my husband and my children and my home."

them, counselors have advised them, and writers have written about them. Women who suffer this problem, in whom this voice is stirring, have lived their whole lives in the pursuit of feminine fulfillment. They are not career women (although career women may have other problems); they are women whose greatest ambition has been marriage and children. For the oldest of these women, these daughters of the American middle class, no other dream was possible. The ones in their forties and fifties who once had other dreams gave them up and threw themselves joyously into life as housewives. For the youngest, the new wives and mothers, this was the only dream. They are the ones who quit high school and college to marry, or marked time in some job in which they had no real interest until they married. These women are very "feminine" in the usual sense, and yet they still suffer the problem.

felt by women preoccupied with desperate problems of hunger, poverty or illness. . . . It is no longer possible today to blame the problem on loss of femininity: to say that education and independence and equality with men have made American women unfeminine. I have heard so many women try to deny this dissatisfied voice within themselves because it does not fit the pretty picture of femininity the experts have given them. I think, in fact, that this is the first clue to the mystery; the problem cannot be understood in the generally accepted terms by which scientists have studied women, doctors have treated

Marshaling a wealth of statistics and first-person accounts, Friedan came to a radical conclusion: The idealized image of the American family was causing irreparable harm to women. According to Friedan, women had been encouraged to confine themselves to the narrow roles of housewife and mother, forsaking education and career aspirations in the process. Friedan attempted to prove that the feminine mystique denied women the opportunity to develop their own identities, which could ultimately lead to problems for women and their families. Friedan saw the feminine mystique as a failed social experiment that the end of World War II and the Cold War helped to create. Women were forced to leave the work world when the soldiers came home from the war and to follow the '50s dictate of "build a better America" by building families.

## NOW BILL OF RIGHTS

The National Organization for Women (NOW) was established on June 30, 1966, in Washington, D.C., by people attending the Third National Conference of the Commission on the Status of Women. Among NOW's twenty-eight founders was its first president, Betty Friedan, and the Rev. Pauli Murray, the first African-American woman Episcopal priest. They coauthored NOW's original Statement of Purpose, which began:

The purpose of NOW is to take action to bring women into full participation in the mainstream of American society now, exercising all privileges and responsibilities thereof in truly equal partnership with men.

One year later, in Washington, D.C., at its first national conference, the organization adopted a bill of rights:

## BILL OF RIGHTS
## We Demand

I. That the U.S. Congress immediately pass the Equal Rights Amendment to the Constitution to provide that "Equality of Rights under the law shall not be denied or abridged by the United States or by any State on account of sex," and that such then be immediately ratified by the several states.

II. That equal employment opportunity be guaranteed to all women, as well as men, by insisting that the Equal Employment Opportunity Commission enforces the prohibition against racial discrimination.

III. That women be protected by law to ensure their rights to return to their jobs within a reasonable time after childbirth without loss of seniority or other accrued benefits, and be paid maternity leave as a form of social security and/or employee benefits.

IV. Immediate revision of tax laws to permit the deduction of home and childcare expenses for working parents.

V. That childcare facilities be established by law on the same basis as parks, libraries, and public schools, ade-quate to the needs of children from the pre-school years through adolescence, as a community resource to be used by all citizens from all income levels.

VI. That the right of women to be educated to their full potential equally with men be secured by Federal and State legislation, eliminating all discrimination and segregation by sex, written and unwritten, at all levels of education, including colleges, graduate and professional schools, loans and fellowships, and Federal and State training programs such as the Jobs Corps.

VII. The right of women in poverty to secure job training, housing, and family allowances on equal terms with men, but without prejudice to a parent's right to remain at home to care for his or her children; revision of welfare legislation and poverty programs which deny women dignity, privacy, and self-respect.

VIII. The right of women to control their own reproductive lives by removing from the penal code laws limiting access to contraceptive information and devices, and by repealing penal laws governing abortion.

## THE PERSONAL IS POLITICAL

Sick and tired of being relegated to stuffing envelopes and preparing meals, fed up with sacrificing for causes that were peripheral to their own lives, angry at being pushed to the sidelines of Vietnam War protests and the Civil Rights Movement simply because of their gender, women involved in radical politics suddenly had a moment of self-awareness. While the men in the organizations dealt with the "real" issues, the women were relegated to "women's work." As they looked around and shared their experiences with each other, they realized their lives were not changing. In her 1970 bestseller *Sisterhood Is Powerful*, editor Robin Morgan wrote:

> Thinking we were involved in the struggle to build a new society, it was a slowly dawning and depressing realization that **we were doing the same work *in* the Movement as out of it;** typing the speeches men delivered; making coffee but not policy, being accessories to the men whose politics would supposedly replace the Old Order.

Protester at the 1968 Miss America Pageant.

# "Miss America Is a Big Falsie."

In fact, their lives appeared to be no different from their mothers'. Their duties were in support of men. They might not be cleaning the house and raising children, but they also were not leading. The radical youth movements they had joined were structured just like the rest of society—male-dominated. While they watched the beliefs and rights of others—from draft-aged males to the poor—being promoted, they started to wonder about their own rights. They began to look at what was happening to each other personally. Out of these feelings of frustration came the battle cry of women's rights: "The Personal Is Political."

Taking a page right out of the African liberation movements that had inspired the Black Panther Party, the women used this battle cry to express their feelings that women's bodies had been colonized by the dominant male culture. Inspired by Frantz Fanon's liberation theory, these newly radicalized feminists—women's liberationists or "libbers"—held that they were members of an oppressed sex class made subordinate by systems of male domination. It was this male culture that was at the core of women's oppression. Unlike liberal feminists, radicals believed that equality should not be the goal. Instead, women needed to seize power through a revolution. In this new utopia, women would reject traditional notions of family, marriage, love, and heterosexuality.

By 1968, many women were leaving the radical political organizations in droves and organizing feminist

# "The Personal Is Political."

groups around the nation. It was out of these groups that the most radical feminists emerged. Among the first of these radical groups to catch the nation's attention were the New York Radical Women. They organized a successful protest of the 1968 Miss America Pageant. On September 7, one hundred women's liberationists descended upon the Atlantic City boardwalk in front of the convention hall. They were there to protest the pageant's promotion of physical attractiveness and charm as the primary attribute of femininity. Mocking the pageant, they crowned a sheep as Miss America and filled a trash barrel—the "Freedom Trash Can"—with symbols of women's bondage: bras, high-heeled shoes, girdles, hair curlers, *Playboy* magazines, false eyelashes, typing books, and more. They planned to burn the contents but were prevented by the police. The spectacle made headlines and the evening news, and though no bras were burned that day, bra burning became the symbol of women's liberation.

After the protest, many of the most extreme participants organized the Redstockings. The name combined the derogatory slang for educated women in the eigh-

## REDSTOCKINGS MANIFESTO (1969)
### published in *Ladies' Home Journal*

I. After centuries of individual and preliminary political struggle, women are united to achieve their final liberation from male supremacy. Redstockings is dedicated to building this unity and winning our freedom.

II. Women are an oppressed class. Our oppression is total, affecting every facet of our lives. We are exploited as sex objects, breeders, domestic servants, and cheap labor. We are considered inferior beings, whose only purpose is to enhance men's lives. Our humanity is denied. Our prescribed behavior is enforced by the threat of physical violence.

Because we have lived so intimately with our oppressors, in isolation from each other, we have been kept from seeing our personal suffering as a political condition. This creates the illusion that a woman's relationship with her man is a matter of interplay between two unique personalities, and can be worked out individually. In reality, every such relationship is a class relationship, and the conflicts between individual men and women are political conflicts that can only be solved collectively.

III. We identify the agents of our oppression as men. Male supremacy is the oldest, most basic form of domination. All other forms of exploitation and oppression (racism, capitalism, imperialism, etc.) are extensions of male supremacy: men dominate women, a few men dominate the rest. All power structures throughout history have been male-dominated and male-oriented. Men have controlled all political, economic and cultural institutions and backed up this control with physical force. They have used their power to keep women in an inferior position. All men receive economic, sexual, and psychological benefits from male supremacy. All men have oppressed women.

IV. Attempts have been made to shift the burden of responsibility from men to institutions or to women themselves. We condemn these arguments as evasions. Institutions alone do not oppress; they are merely tools of the oppressor. To blame institutions implies that men and women are equally victimized, obscures the fact that men benefit from the subordination of women, and gives men the excuse that they are forced to be oppressors. On the contrary, any man is free to renounce his superior position provided that he is willing to be treated like a woman by other men.

We also reject the idea that women consent to or are to blame for their own oppression. Women's submission

teenth and nineteenth centuries, "bluestockings," with the color of radical politics, "red." Though the organization lasted only a few short years, it influenced the debate on women's rights greatly. The Redstockings first appeared in 1969 at a New York City legislative hearing on abortion law reform. At the hearing, they tried to take over the microphone when only twelve speakers—eleven men and a nun—were scheduled.

They went on to occupy the offices of the *Ladies' Home Journal* to demand that they be allowed to put out a "liberated" issue and that the magazine replace the male editor and publisher. The magazine, which had a 6.9 million circulation, agreed to let them publish a special section.

is not the result of brainwashing, stupidity, or mental illness but of continual, daily pressure from men. We do not need to change our-selves, but to change men.

The most slanderous evasion of all is that women can oppress men. The basis for this illusion is the isolation of individual relationships from their political context and the tendency of men to see any legitimate challenge to their privileges as persecution.

V. We regard our personal experience, and our feelings about that experience, as the basis for an analysis of our common situation. We cannot rely on existing ideologies as they are all products of male supremacist culture. We question every generalization and accept none that are not confirmed by our experience.

Our chief task at present is to develop female class consciousness through sharing experience and publicly exposing the sexist foundation of all our institutions. Consciousness-raising is not "therapy," which implies the existence of individual solutions and falsely assumes that the male-female relationship is purely personal, but the only method by which we can ensure that our program for liberation is based on the concrete realities of our lives.

The first requirement for raising class consciousness

is honesty, in private and in public, with ourselves and other women.

VI. We identify with all women. We define our best interest as that of the poorest, most brutally exploited woman.

We repudiate all economic, racial, educational or status privileges that divide us from other women. We are determined to recognize and eliminate any prejudices we may hold against other women.

We are committed to achieving internal democracy. We will do whatever is necessary to ensure that every woman in our movement has an equal chance to participate, assume responsibility, and develop her political potential.

VII. We call on all our sisters to unite with us in struggle.

We call on all men to give up their male privileges and support women's liberation in the interest of our humanity and their own.

In fighting for our liberation we will always take the side of women against their oppressors. We will not ask what is "revolutionary" or "reformist," only what is good for women.

The time for individual skirmishes has passed. This time we are going all the way.

# "Sisterhood Is Powerful."

## ERA

In 1972, Congress passed the Equal Rights Amendment, which outlawed any gender discrimination in all aspects of American life, and sent it to the states for ratification. Thirty-five states passed the amendment, but it fell three states short of being ratified and amended to the Constitution. Supporters of the amendment believed it was essential in order for men and women to be equal in all aspects of American life, particularly in the workplace. Opponents feared a number of things, including the undermining of special protections women receive under the law and the destruction of the traditional roles men and women play in families. The debate on this amendment highlighted just how much '60s activism had split the country on fundamental questions about justice and how to attain it.

## OUR BODIES, OURSELVES

In 1969, Norma, Pam, Judy, Nancy, Paula, Ruth, Wilma, Esther, Jane, Wendy, and Joan gathered in a small room to talk about their health. They were attending a women's liberation conference in Boston. The conference was one of the first gatherings of women to meet and talk about their lives and health. Each of these women had signed up for the workshop "Control of Our Bodies," which was being led by Nancy. As each shared her experiences with doctors and her knowledge—or lack thereof—about her body, a surprising consensus began to arise. "We had all experienced similar feelings of frustration and anger toward specific doctors and the medical maze in general, and we initially wanted to do something about those doctors who were condescending, paternalistic, judgmental and noninformative," remembered the women.

**Anti-ERA demonstrators**

As the workshop ended, they decided they didn't want the discussion to end. They formed a study group, which they called the Doctor's Group, and committed to meeting regularly to discuss women's health topics. Their initial goal was simply to know more about themselves. They lived in a culture where women were not supposed to talk about their bodies because it was shameful, and doctors did not share what they knew about women's health. It was a culture where women were passive and were expected to accept a doctor's authority.

What surprised—and, more important, empowered— these women was their discovery that they knew as much, if not more, about themselves as their doctors. Outside of reproductive health, the medical profession treated their bodies as if they were simply men with breasts. All of the women were college-educated, mostly white, and mostly middle-class, but they had all been indoctrinated into the myth that medical information was too complex for them

**"From the start, our goals have been to share information, empower ourselves and one another, to make connections with one another..."**

*Our Bodies, Ourselves* **has been banned by high schools and public libraries across the country. Jerry Falwell, the conservative founder of the Moral Majority, famously condemned the book as "obscene trash."**

**Original members of the Doctor's Group**

"In my heart, I think a woman has two choices: either she's a feminist or a masochist."

—Gloria Steinem

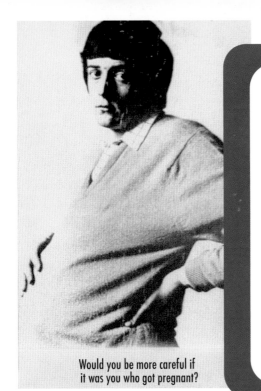

Would you be more careful if it was you who got pregnant?

**ROE V. WADE** For many feminists, the landmark 1973 Supreme Court decision guaranteeing a woman's right to abortion in the first trimester of her pregnancy was the single most important achievement in their movement. It guaranteed that women had control of their bodies and could make decisions about their health without the interference of outside parties. The ruling was in response to a 1969 class-action suit brought in Texas by Norma McCorvey (under the pseudonym "Jane Roe") against Texas district attorney Henry Wade. The court ruled that the "right to privacy" expressed in the Fourteenth and Ninth Amendments was "broad enough to encompass a woman's decision to terminate her pregnancy."

In the 1960s, a woman had to get permission from her husband to have a tubal ligation, a procedure that made pregnancy impossible. Single women were generally refused such procedures.

to understand. What they discovered was that technical research and medical documents were not above their heads.

At the time, there were virtually no books on women's health issues for women to read. When they began meeting weekly, the women shared what research they could with one another and began to teach themselves about women's health issues. They covered even basic issues that were not widely known then, such as the function of the clitoris as a source of a woman's personal pleasure. It didn't take long for the group to realize that women's health knowledge was important to share with women everywhere.

The group's first lecture was titled "Sexuality" and was scheduled at the Massachusetts Institute of Technology, a traditionally male institution. The event was advertised by word of mouth and drew more than fifty women. Before the year was out, the Doctor's Group had gathered their talks into book form. The small, radical New England Free Press published *Women and Their Bodies*, a 193-page booklet that was printed on newsprint and stapled. With almost no marketing, the booklet sold more than a quarter of a million copies.

This breakthrough and success was only the beginning. In 1972, the same group of women incorporated as the Boston Women's Health Book Collective (BWHBC) and published the book with Simon & Schuster the following year. From the beginning, BWHBC was at the forefront of women's health issues. They demonstrated for abortion rights. They publicized horrendous medical practices, such as the fact that a large percentage of women in Puerto Rico were sterilized without their knowledge. They urged women to go in pairs to doctors in order to ensure that they received answers to their questions.

"From the start, our goals have been to share information, empower ourselves and one another, to make connections with one another, to create preventative-health alternatives, to improve health policies relevant to women and to work on changing the system to meet our needs," writes Jane Pincus, a cofounder.

To that end, they've stirred an enormous amount of controversy. Their 1973 edition included the chapter "In America, They Call Us Dykes," which was one of the first pieces in support of women loving women. Later, they included chapters on the international exploitation of women and translated the book into dozens of languages. In 1976, *Our Bodies, Ourselves* was recognized by the American Library Association's Young Adult Library Services Association as one of the best books of the decade.

# UPSIDE-DOWN FLAG

**P**eople are fighting battles in the streets of Chicago. They're fighting to stop the Vietnam War and bring about changes in the political party system. They're fighting in the streets of Alabama to change the situation for blacks. The SDS movement is trying to change the whole structure of the universities. What the hell are we going to do? Are we going to sit here in Minnesota and not do a goddamn thing? Are we going to go on for another two hundred years, or even another five, the way we are without doing something for our Indian people?

"What treaty that the whites
have kept has the red man broken?

Not one.

What treaty that the white man
ever made with us have they kept?

Not one."

—Sitting Bull

On the hot summer evening of July 28, 1968, Dennis Banks, who had recently finished a stint in prison for robbery, spoke these words to open a meeting in the basement of a local Minneapolis church. The basement was filled with around two hundred other Native Americans, but Banks's words resonated particularly with three other ex-convicts—Eddie Benton Benai, George Mitchell, and Clyde Bellecourt.

In the '60s most Native-American adult males were in jail, on parole, or under supervision, or had been in the past. In his memoir, *Ojibwa Warrior*, Banks describes the environment with dripping irony:

**Together with the first robin came the annual renewal of the "quota system," which meant that the police had to arrest a certain number of Indians—usually about two hundred a week—to provide unpaid labor for the work house and various city projects. ...During the early sixties I got caught in that dragnet maybe twenty-five times....For Indians, doing time in jail is almost a traditional rite of passage.**

America treated Native Americans as if they were scum. Over the previous three decades, they had been subject to a systematic attempt by the government to destroy their culture. Their children were removed from their homes on reservations and placed in boarding schools, where their hair was cut, they were forbidden to speak their native tongue, and their history was ignored. At the same time, the government relocated thousands of Native Americans off their reservations into cities like Minneapolis/St. Paul, Los Angeles, and Portland, Oregon. After living on isolated reservations, they had no experience negotiating the complex requirements of surviving in an urban environment. Quickly, these new urban enclaves came to be known as "red slums," where Indians held the lowest-level jobs and

were denied education and decent housing. In short, the government was trying to systematically destroy what little was left of Native-American culture.

It was in this environment that these ex-convict Native Americans committed themselves to creating a civil rights organization for Indians. Clyde Bellecourt was elected chairman of the group. They initially called themselves the "Concerned Indian Americans," but the irony of its initials—CIA—was quickly realized and within days they settled on a name with more appealing initials: the American Indian Movement, or AIM.

Cofounder Dennis Banks summed up their hopes for AIM ...

Dennis Banks

"We started here in the Twin Cities, but from the start,
our Movement was based on the guarantees to Indians in all the treaties;
we didn't want to get caught up in the civil rights struggle because that
was between blacks and whites; it was within the System,
and the System had nothing to do with Indians."

—AIM cofounder Clyde Bellecourt

## 1960S NATIVE-AMERICAN POPULATION STATISTICS

Because of poverty and a system that dealt harshly with them, Native Americans disproportionately were imprisoned in western states and Canada.

| | % OF TOTAL POPULATION | % OF PRISON POPULATION |
|---|---|---|
| Minnesota | 1% | 8% |
| South Dakota | 6.5% | 25–33% |

Because of the slum housing conditions; the highest unemployment rate in the whole of this country; police brutality against our elders, women, and children; Native Warriors came together from the streets, prisons, jails and the urban ghettos of Minneapolis to form the American Indian Movement. They were tired of begging for welfare, tired of being scapegoats in America and decided to start building on the strengths of our own people; decided to build our own schools; our own job training programs; and our own destiny. That was our motivation to begin. That beginning is now being called "the Era of Indian Power."

At first, they took a page right out of the Black Panther strategy book and formed an Indian patrol, wearing identical red berets, to protect their community against the police. Unlike the Panthers, however, the Indian patrol used nonviolent strategies and carried cameras and tape recorders instead of guns. By filming arrests and advising those taken into custody that they did not have to plead guilty, that they were entitled to an attorney and a jury trial, Indian arrests and convictions dropped dramatically. The hostility by police and other authorities, however, increased instead of decreased. Over this period, Bellecourt was beaten more than thirty times and received a broken jaw by the police. The newly formed civil rights group also organized social services to help their community find adequate jobs, housing, and education. Their initial focus was simply improving the lives of Native Americans living in urban areas.

Local authorities and the FBI immediately considered AIM a violent terrorist group in the vein of the Black Panther Party. It was clear that authorities for some reason could not get past their own biases. They looked at the members of AIM as criminals because they had committed crimes. Rather than recognizing AIM's activism as a positive, they saw AIM's efforts to improve their community as a threat.

## NATIONAL INDIAN YOUTH COUNCIL

In 1960, Vine Deloria Jr. and other educated young Indians founded the first all-Indian protest group. They staged "fish-ins" to act on their treaty rights. These actions began at a popular fishing place known as Frank's Landing in Puget Sound and confronted authorities who wanted to limit Native-American fishing rights because of white overfishing.

"The poorest of the poor—by far—are the Indian people. It is true that in our courts today the Indian has legal status as a citizen, but anyone familiar with Indian life, in cities or on reservations, can testify that justice for Indians is random and arbitrary where it exists at all."

—Peter Matthiessen,
*In the Spirit of Crazy Horse*

By 1973, AIM had seventy-nine chapters, eight of which were in Canada.

Not surprisingly, the harder the authorities pushed the new group, the more belligerent and hostile the group became. The confrontational approach simply reinforced centuries-long feelings of being oppressed by the U.S. government—whether local or federal, it did not really matter. This drew new members to the cause and helped encourage AIM to expand its mission beyond simply helping urban Native Americans. As it grew, AIM became committed to restoring the lands that the government stole after signing treaties and committed to reclaiming the language, religion, and culture of its people. With this broadening of expectations came a dramatic shift in strategy.

"We questioned our beliefs about 'necessary violence' and whether we should arm ourselves," said Dennis Banks. "I didn't want AIM to be seen as a group that advocated violence, but, on the other hand, I felt that our people should not face heavily armed, racist cops empty-handed. There was just too much evidence of racism in the streets, and sometimes a show of strength can prevent violence."

At a rally in Wisconsin, AIM adopted the upside-down American flag as its symbol because it was the international signal for people in distress. "No one could deny that Indians were in bad trouble and needed help," said Banks.

### WE HOLD THE ROCK!

"We hold the rock!" came the cry across San Francisco Bay on the afternoon of November 20, 1969. This roar was extraordinary not simply because approximately 100 Native Americans had occupied Alcatraz Island, the notorious federal penitentiary closed five years earlier. Perhaps more incredible was that the call came from a group of young urban Indian college students who hailed from

# INDIANS OF ALL NATIONS

## THE ALCATRAZ PROCLAMATION
### to the
### Great White Father and his People

### 1969

Fellow citizens, we are asking you to join with us in our attempt to better the lives of all Indian people.

We are on Alcatraz Island to make known to the world that we have a right to use our land for our own benefit.

In a proclamation of November 20, 1969, we told the government of the United States that we are here "to create a meaningful use for our Great Spirit's Land."

We, the native Americans, reclaim the land known as Alcatraz Island in the name of all American Indians by right of discovery.

We wish to be fair and honorable in our dealings with the Caucasian inhabitants of this land, and hereby offer the following treaty:

**We will purchase said Alcatraz Island for twenty-four dollars in glass beads and red cloth, a precedent set by the white man's purchase of a similar island about 300 years ago. We know that $24 in trade goods for these 16 acres is more than was paid when Manhattan Island was sold, but we know that land values have risen over the years. Our offer of $1.24 per acre is greater than the $0.47 per acre the white men are now paying the California Indians for their lands....**

different tribes. They called themselves "Indians of All Tribes" and were the first to unite Native Americans from different tribes to work together against the injustices committed by the U.S. government. Prior to Alcatraz, Indian activism had been generally tribal in nature, centered in small geographic areas and focused on specific issues, such as illegal trespass or fishing rights.

Occupying Alcatraz was the brainchild of Richard Oakes, a young charismatic Mohawk Indian and college student in the Bay area. He was inspired by an earlier occupation on March 9, 1964, led by Richard McKenzie and four other Sioux. McKenzie and his group stayed only four hours, but their demands for the use of the island for a cultural center and an Indian university resonated with Oakes.

On November 9, 1969, Oakes, along with Indian stu-

dents he had met at the American Indian Studies Center at UCLA and Bay area urban Indians, symbolically occupied the island. They claimed the island in the name of the Indians of all tribes and departed that evening. Afterward, Oakes and the others realized that they actually could take hold of the island. Over the following week, they organized a long-term occupation of Alcatraz Island. On November 20, these young urban Indian students climbed into a chartered boat, the *Monte Cristo*, and made their way across San Francisco Bay to Alcatraz.

These idealistic men and women quickly began to organize, electing a council and giving everyone on the island a job: security, sanitation, cooking, and laundry. All decisions were made by unanimous consent. For the first few days, this remarkable utopian community worked well, but as the resistance from the federal government to

**Protest graffiti on Alcatraz**

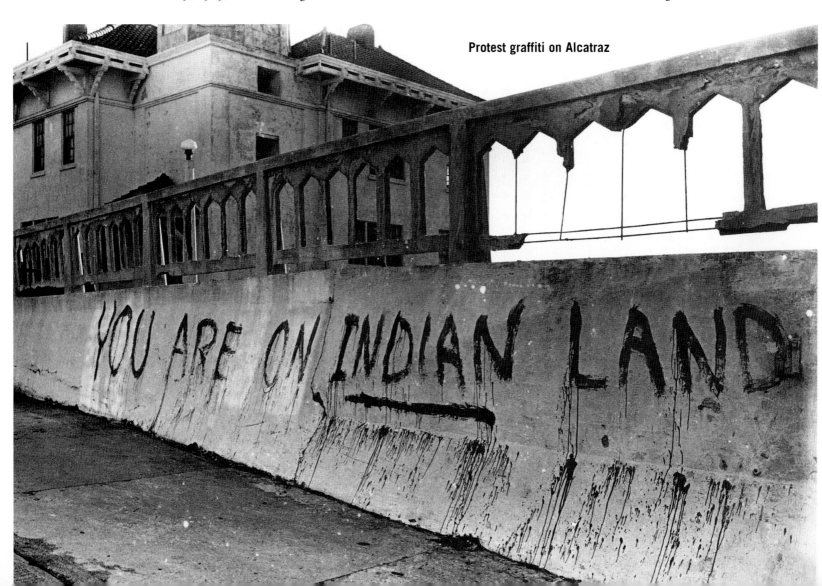

# "As a result of the occupation...the official government policy of termination of Indian tribes was ended..."

★ ★ ★ ★ ★ ★ ★ ★ ★ ★ ★ ★ ★ ★ ★ ★ ★ ★ ★ ★ ★ ★ ★ ★ ★

their demands continued and the weeks passed, the organization could not hold. Many of the students began returning to school in January 1970 and were replaced by less disciplined participants from urban areas and reservations. As the news spread of the occupation, others, non-Indians, also began arriving on the island. Many were involved in the hippie and drug culture of San Francisco and looked at the occupation as an opportunity to have a party.

When tragedy occurred on January 5, the organizers were shattered. Richard Oakes's thirteen-year-old step-daughter, Yvonne, fell three floors to her death within the prison. Oakes immediately departed, and competing groups began to battle for leadership.

Perhaps wisely, the government decided to wait the insurgents out. The FBI and Coast Guard surrounded the island but did not remove anyone or prevent anyone from landing on Alcatraz. In some ways this strategy incited the protesters even more. Time and again over the decade, when the government turned a blind eye to protests against its policies, protesters became more radical. This happened when the younger members of the Civil Rights Movement morphed into the Black Panther Party, and again when the more radical members of the SDS broke away to form the Weathermen. The government in its vast and sprawling bureaucracy could not see the pattern, but it was there.

As no progress was made in meeting their demands, the remaining protesters on Alcatraz Island became more entrenched. By June, nothing less than full title to the island and the establishment of a university and cultural center would end the siege. In response to this hardening

of their position, the government cut off electricity and clean water to the island. At this point, a fire broke out and several historic buildings were destroyed. Whatever organization there had been now devolved into chaos, and there was no visible leadership with which the government would negotiate.

As the situation became more desperate on the island, people began looting, stripping copper wiring and copper tubing from the buildings and selling it as scrap metal. Finally, on June 10, 1971, one and a half years after the initial occupation, armed federal marshals, FBI agents, and special forces police launched an attack on the island and removed five women, four children, and six unarmed Indian men. With this action, the occupation ended.

It is ironic and sad in some ways how extreme measures almost always fail but often empower more moderate groups to take up the broader cause and change society. Historian Troy Johnson in his essay "The Alcatraz Indian Occupation" summed up the action this way:

> The success or failure of the occupation should not be judged by whether the demands of the occupiers were realized. The underlying goals of the Indians on Alcatraz were to awaken the American public to the reality of the plight of the first Americans and to assert the need for Indian self-determination. As a result of the occupation, either directly or indirectly, the official government policy of termination of Indian tribes was ended and a policy of Indian self-determination became the official U.S. government policy.

While the island was occupied, President Nixon made

a dramatic shift in policy. He returned Blue Lake and 48,000 acres of land to the Taos Indians. Eventually, an Indian university was created near Davis, California. In the bigger picture, Indians might have lost the battle on Alcatraz, but they clearly won the war, giving birth to a political movement.

## TRAIL OF BROKEN TREATIES
### Maybe we should do something like the Civil Rights Movement's 1963 March on Washington.
—*Native-American activist*

The success and failure of the Alcatraz occupation provided a catalyst to broader and more ambitious action by many young Native Americans. By 1972, AIM had transformed itself from a local advocacy group organized to monitor the daily harassment of Indians by the Minneapolis police into the nation's most visible Indian rights organization. Their mission expanded dramatically:

- Challenge Indian killings by whites.
- Speak out about treaty rights.
- Promote traditional culture.
- Organize survival schools to teach heritage and religion.
- Sponsor religious ceremonies.

It was at a Sun Dance ceremony on the Rosebud Sioux reservation the summer of 1972 that the idea for a march on Washington was first mentioned. Within months, momentum grew and a cross-country caravan starting at three separate points on the West Coast was organized. Called the "Trail of Broken Treaties" (TBT), the march was to pick up Indians along the way and arrive in Washington, D.C., right before the 1972 presidential elections.

A long parade of old cars and trucks arrived

★ ★

**PREAMBLE TO TRAIL OF BROKEN TREATIES
20-POINT POSITION PAPER**

## AN INDIAN MANIFESTO FOR RESTITUTION, REPARATIONS, RESTORATION OF LANDS FOR A RECONSTRUCTION OF AN INDIAN FUTURE IN AMERICA

### THE TRAIL OF BROKEN TREATIES

We need not give another recitation of past complaints nor engage in redundant dialogue of discontent. Our conditions and their cause for being should perhaps be best known by those who have written the record of America's action against Indian people. In 1832, Black Hawk correctly observed: You know the cause of our making war. It is known to all white men. They ought to be ashamed of it.

The government of the United States knows the reasons for our going to its capital city. Unfortunately, they don't know how to greet us. We go because America has been only too ready to express shame, and suffer none from the expression—while remaining wholly unwilling to change to allow life for Indian people.

We seek a new American majority—a majority that is not content merely to confirm itself by superiority in numbers, but which by conscience is committed toward prevailing upon the public will in ceasing wrongs and in doing right. For our part, in words and deeds of coming days, we propose to produce a rational, reasoned manifesto for construction of an Indian future in America. If America has maintained faith with its original spirit, or may recognize it now, we should not be denied.

AMERICA DREAMING

November 2, five days before the election, bearing bumper stickers such as CUSTER HAD IT COMING, AND SO DO SOME OTHERS, REMEMBER CRAZY HORSE, and UNITED STATES IS INDIAN COUNTRY. They came with a twenty-point plan for "securing an Indian future in America" (left).

As hundreds of Indians arrived in the city, they had no place to stay. The Indians gathered in the Bureau of Indian Affairs (BIA) auditorium, where they camped. Quickly, things got out of hand and a group of young Indians seized the BIA building. They barricaded the doors, blocked the windows, and upended desks. Sheets bearing NATIVE AMERICAN EMBASSY were hung from the windows.

First, the government tried to broker a quick negotiation for the release of the building. After negotiations failed, the Nixon Administration panicked. The last thing they wanted was bad publicity just days before the election. On Monday, November 6, they convinced a judge to order the forcible removal of Indians by 6 p.m. that evening. In response, the young Indians holding the building lost control. The building was trashed. They threatened to set the building on fire by 5:45 p.m. if nothing positive occurred or if they saw police movement.

Staff members from the White House forced their way into the BIA building at 5:30 p.m. and negotiated a truce in which the White House counsel, the Office of Management and Budget director, and the Secretary of the Interior would negotiate directly with the Indians. By election morning, a meeting was held and a federal task force was agreed upon to examine wide issues in Indian country. As well, amnesty was promised and money for transportation home was allocated. A sigh of relief could be heard as Nixon won the presidential election.

Not everyone was happy with the agreement, and the

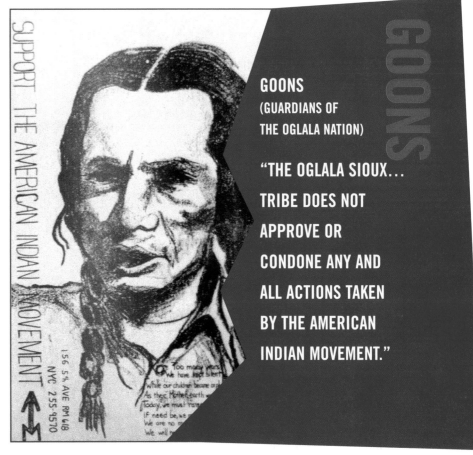

GOONS
(GUARDIANS OF
THE OGLALA NATION)

"THE OGLALA SIOUX... TRIBE DOES NOT APPROVE OR CONDONE ANY AND ALL ACTIONS TAKEN BY THE AMERICAN INDIAN MOVEMENT."

Nixon administration would come to regret their capitulation. The consequences of the action did not simply embarrass the U.S. government but also split what had seemed like a unified Indian nation. Dick Wilson, tribal chairman of the Oglala Sioux and leader of a corrupt group called GOONS, wired the government: "THE OGLALA SIOUX...TRIBE DOES NOT APPROVE OR CONDONE ANY AND ALL ACTIONS TAKEN BY THE AMERICAN INDIAN MOVEMENT." These words left the government feeling humiliated. What started out as a triumph of unification ended up tearing the Indian nations and the government apart. "Alcatraz had been tolerated, then ended in time to avoid conflict with the election. Then these same Indians invaded the capitol on election eve. The next time, there would be no toleration. In the White House's own words, these were twentieth-century 'renegades,'" wrote historian Kenneth S. Stern in his acclaimed *Loud Hawk: The United States Versus the American Indian Movement.*

## BURY MY HEART AT WOUNDED KNEE

The whites are crazy!
The whites are crazy!
—*ghost-dance song*

**March 1, 1973 Presidential News Summary:**
U.S. officers sealed off the entire Oglala Sioux reservation where about 300 militants of Amer. Indian Movement seized Wounded Knee, SD, and took 10 hostages and exchanged fire w/officers.... All nets noted trading post was stripped of food, clothes, gun and Indian relics as Indians who say they'll die for cause attempted to force attention on what they say is corruption and mismanagement w/in BIA.

**March 3, 1973 Presidential News Summary:**
CBS w/ominous film of Indians fixing sights on weapons and Armored Personnel Carriers (APCs) in area. Meanwhile food supplies of Indians and villagers are dwindling.

**March 5, 1973 Presidential News Summary:**
"Tension grows worse every day," said a typically ominous report on NBC Sunday.... "Another showdown is in the making at Wounded Knee," said NBC Sat. where gov't's "flexing of the muscles" w/the APCs was featured along w/Molotov cocktails and "fortresses" being built by the hopelessly outmanned Indians faced by gov't demands for "unconditional surrender."

These reports that President Nixon received in the Oval Office were referring to the February 27 occupation of Wounded Knee, South Dakota, on the Pine Ridge Reservation by approximately 200 Sioux.

The occupation was a spontaneous uprising that came when a meeting organized by traditional Chief Frank Fools Crow was moved from a community building that was too small for the large crowd to a larger hall across the reservation. On the way to the other hall, the caravan of vehicles passed through Wounded Knee, site of the infamous massacre of 300 Sioux by the U.S. Seventh Cavalry in 1890.

In the months leading up to the 1973 siege, Pine Ridge was torn between supporters of AIM and followers of the corrupt tribal government under Dick Wilson. Frequent acts of violence ranging from beatings to murders erupted regularly between the groups. Wilson had organized a special police force, commonly known as GOON squads (Guardians of the Oglala Nation), and used them as his private army to intimidate the people living on the reservation. AIM members and supporters felt persecuted and threatened.

"...nobody is recognizing th

**114**

It was in this atmosphere on the evening of February 27 that AIM members and supporters finally decided to take a stand. As they passed through the tiny village of Wounded Knee, the tragic history of persecution resonated with the group. At that moment the symbolic power of Wounded Knee seemed like the ideal reason to take a stand. The caravan stopped and took over the village, holding eleven allies of the tribal president hostage. Within hours, local authorities and federal agents, who were responsible for law enforcement on reservations, descended. The next day, the Sioux traded gunfire with the federal marshals surrounding Wounded Knee, and AIM leader Russell Means began negotiations for the release of the hostages, demanding that the U.S. Senate launch an investigation of the Bureau of Indian Affairs, Pine Ridge, and all Sioux reservations in South Dakota, and that the Senate Committee on Foreign Relations hold hearings on the scores of Indian treaties broken by the U.S. government.

The Wounded Knee occupation lasted for a total of seventy days, during which time two Sioux men were shot to death by federal agents. One federal agent was paralyzed after being shot. On May 8, the AIM leaders and their supporters surrendered after White House officials promised to investigate their complaints. The AIM leaders were arrested, but on September 16, 1973, a federal judge dismissed the charges against them because of the U.S. government's unlawful handling of witnesses and evidence.

Violence continued on the Pine Ridge Reservation throughout the rest of the 1970s, with several more AIM members and supporters losing their lives in confrontations with the U.S. government. The government took no steps to honor broken Indian treaties. Nevertheless, like other civil rights groups, Native Americans won in the courts and won major settlements from federal and state governments in cases involving tribal land claims.

Russell Means, AIM leader at Wounded Knee:

"This is our last gasp as a sovereign people. And if we don't get these treaty rights recognized, as equal to the Constitution of the United States—as by law they are—then you might as well kill me, because I have no reason for living. And that's why I'm here in Wounded Knee, because nobody is recognizing the Indian people as human beings....

We haven't demanded any radical changes here, only that the United States Government live up to its own laws. It is precedent-setting that a group of 'radicals,' who in the minds of some are acting outside the law, are just in turn asking the law to live up to its own. We're not asking for any radical changes. We're just asking for the law to be equitably applied—to all."

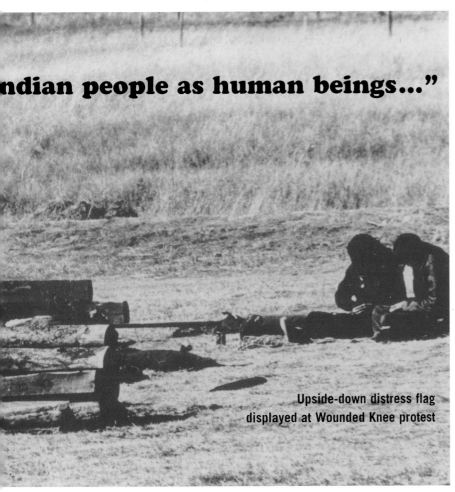
ndian people as human beings..."

Upside-down distress flag displayed at Wounded Knee protest

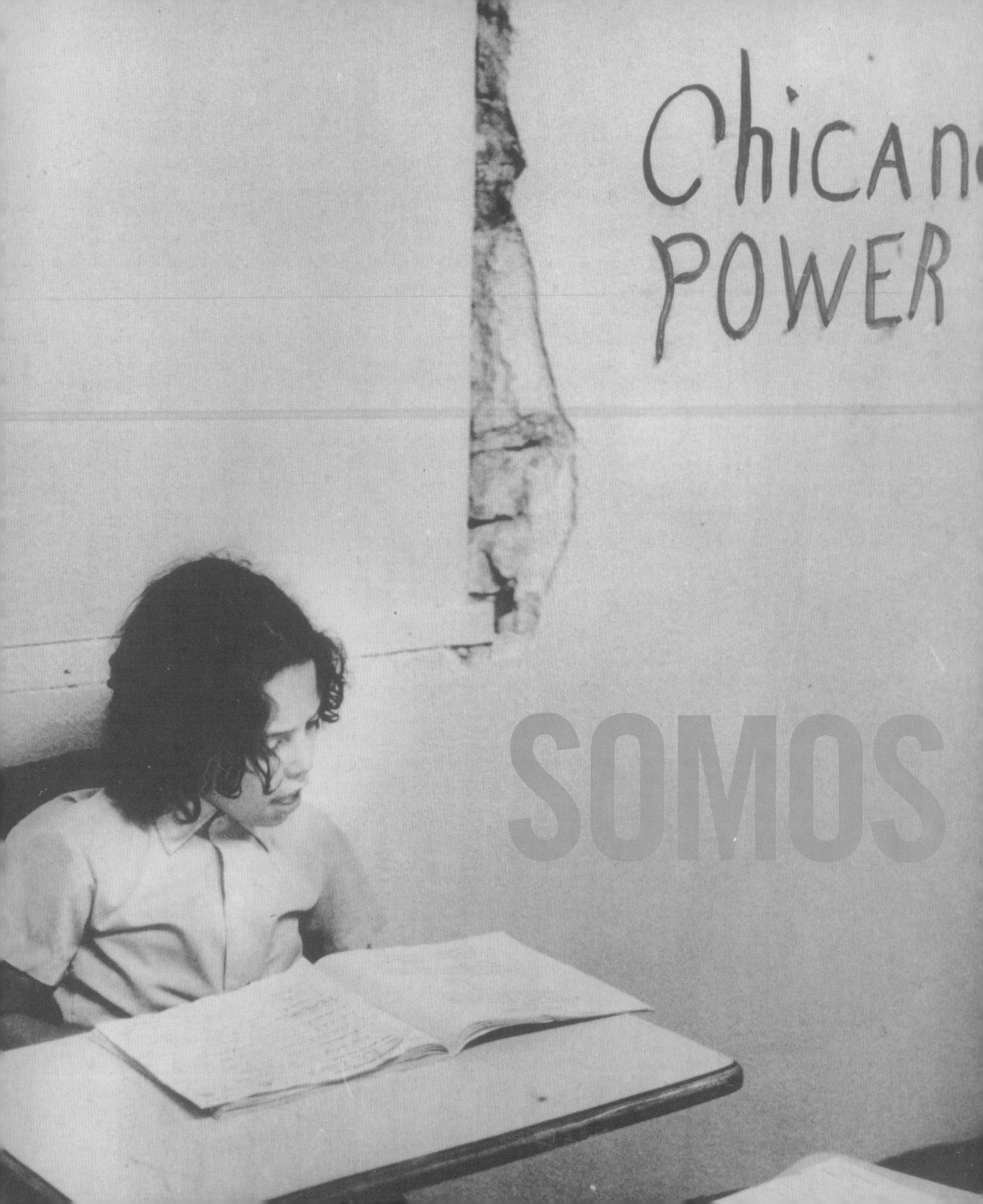


SOMOS

# EMPOWERING MEXICAN AMERICANS AND PUERTO RICANS

## I Am Joaquín

I am Joaquín

lost in a world of confusion,

caught up in the whirl of a gringo society,

confused by the rules,

scorned by attitudes,

suppressed by manipulation,

and destroyed by modern society.

# LATINOS

When Rodolfo "Corky" Gonzáles put these words to the page in 1967, it seemed as if for the first time someone was writing of all the frustration and hurt young Mexican Americans had been feeling for some time. America was a country that was defined along the racial lines of black and white. "Joaquín" spoke of a people who did not fit in this archetype, but existed somewhere in between...in a place that was brown.

My fathers have lost the economic battle and won
    the struggle of cultural survival.
And now! I must choose between the paradox of
Victory of the spirit, despite physical hunger
Or

to exist in the grasp of American social neurosis,
sterilization of the soul, and a full stomach.
YES,
I have come a long way to nowhere, Unwillingly
    dragged by that
monstrous, technical industrial giant called
Progress and Anglo success...
I look at myself. I watch my brothers.
I shed tears of sorrow.
I sow seeds of hate.
I withdraw to the safety within the
Circle of life...
MY OWN PEOPLE

In his groundbreaking poem "I Am Joaquín," Gonzáles struck a deep, emotional chord by defining a culture that had never been explicitly defined until then. The poem was quickly mimeographed and circulated among the Mexican-American community. It spread like a virus among the nascent Mexican-American student organizations on campuses across the Southwest and West.

It was only a few years earlier that these student organizations had begun to form. Mexican Americans had participated in civil rights protests. Most notably, Maria Varela became a key SNCC organizer in Alabama, where she established an adult literacy project. She was a cofounder of SDS at the University of Michigan. Elizabeth Sutherland Martinez, a civil rights activist of Mexican descent, became director of the New York City SNCC office in 1964 and also worked in Mississippi. Others participated in the march on Washington organized by King and the SCLC in 1963, while a few Latinos joined a campus protest when a black student was denied admission at San José State College. Still, the relationship between the Civil Rights Movement and Latino rights seemed remote, not just for Mexican Americans but for the country as a whole. President Johnson's War on Poverty initially did not address poverty in the barrios.

In response, Mexican-American student organizations began to form to speak out explicitly about Latin issues. Two of the first were MAYO, Mexican American Youth Organization, at St. Mary's College in San Antonio, Texas, and MASO, Mexican American Student Organization, at the University of Texas at Austin. Quickly, chapters of UMAS, United Mexican American Students, were formed at UCLA, California State College, Loyola University, USC, California State College at Long Beach, and San

# Mexican Americans needed to lay claim to their cultural identity in order to have the pride to demand their civil rights.

Fernando State College. Then MASA, Mexican American Student Association, came together at East Los Angeles Community College.

In 1965, they found a collective voice. Rodolfo "Corky" Gonzáles, a retired boxer, organized the Crusade for Justice, the first Mexican-American civil rights organization in Denver, Colorado. It was out of this work that he was inspired to write "I Am Joaquín." He believed that Mexican Americans needed to lay claim to their cultural identity in order to have the pride to demand their civil rights.

I am the Eagle and Serpent of the Aztec civilization.
I owned the land as far as the eye could see under
    the crown of Spain,
and I toiled on my earth and gave my Indian sweat
    and blood for the Spanish master,
Who ruled with tyranny over man and beast and all
    that he could trample
But...

THE GROUND WAS MINE.
I was both tyrant and slave.

"I Am Joaquín" did not offer a well-defined radical ideology, but it did provide a framework for the developing student movement through its portrayal of the quest for identity and its critique of racism.

## LA HUELGA AND TIERRA AMARILLA

Two other events conspired to bring Mexican-American youth together. First came "La Huelga," the strike. In 1965, a five-foot-six shy but determined Mexican American led his small fledgling union on a strike against the grape growers in Delano, California. César Chávez had worked for years to start a union for migrant workers. By the mid-'60s he had enlisted around 1,700 families to join his United Farm Workers of America and persuaded two growers to raise wages moderately, but he knew the

**Corky Gonzáles**

1968 HIGH SCHOOL
DROPOUT RATES

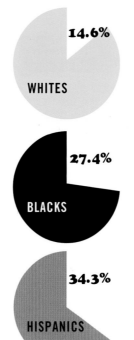

14.6%
WHITES

27.4%
BLACKS

34.3%
HISPANICS

According to the 1960 census, Mexican Americans made up only 2.3 percent of the U.S. population but 12 percent of the populations of Texas, New Mexico, Arizona, Colorado, and California—almost 3.5 million people.

## from the book *Brown* by Richard Rodriguez

Brown as impurity.

I write of a color that is not a singular color, not a strict recipe, not an expected result, but a color produced by careless desire, even by accident; by two or several. I write of blood that is blended. I write of brown as complete freedom of substance and narrative. I extol impurity....

I write about race in America in hopes of undermining the notion of race in America....

Brown is the color most people in the United States associate with Latin America.

Apart from stool sample, there is no browner smear in the American imagination than the Rio Grande. No adjective has attracted itself more often to the Mexican in America than "dirty"—which I assume gropes toward the simile "dirt-like," indicating dense concentrations of melanin.

I am dirty all right. In Latin America, what makes me brown is that I am made of the conquistador and the Indian. My brown is a reminder of conflict.

And of reconciliation.

workers were too weak for a strike. There were more than 100,000 migrant workers in California; if his small group went on strike, growers easily would be able to find other migrants to replace them.

The decision to strike was made for him, however. An even smaller union, the AFL-CIO Agricultural Workers Organizing Committtee, with about 800 members, struck against grape growers in Delano. Chávez's members immediately wanted to join the strike. Reluctantly, Chávez agreed, afraid that they would be crushed and his union destroyed. Nevertheless, he led his union into the fight.

Like Martin Luther King Jr., Chávez was a follower of Gandhi and nonviolence. He had witnessed what it had done for the moral authority of the Civil Rights Movement. As he and his small labor union stood in defiance of the all-powerful grape growers, the union seemed like David taking on the Goliath that was agriculture. He inspired nuns and priests, union leaders, and students to join him in Delano. In 1967, he was the first Mexican-American leader to appear on the cover of *Time*. In 1968, Chávez began his most successful campaign, urging consumers not to buy grapes grown in the San Joaquin Valley until the growers agreed to union contracts. The boycott proved a huge success when more than 17 million Americans stopped buying grapes because of the boycott. On July 30, 1970, after losing millions of dollars, growers agreed to sign a contract. It was probably the high point in the union's history.

Chávez, however, considered himself a labor leader, not a leader in the fight for Mexican-American rights. His interest was in improving the lives of migrant workers of all national origins, including Filipino, Japanese, Mexican American, and Native American, among others. To student activists like Armando Valdez, this was a clear disappointment. Valdez graduated from San José State College, where he was one of the founders of a Mexican-American student organization. After college, he traveled to Cuba, where he found inspiration in Castro's revolution. Next he joined the San Francisco Mime Troupe and participated in its brand of political theater, but when the grape strike began in 1965, Valdez moved to Delano and founded the Teatro Campesino, a political theater group that promoted not so much a new idea but an old idea in a fresh and provocative way—Chicano identity. By the mid-'60s, Mexican-American youths were beginning to call themselves Chicanos to distinguish themselves from their elders and to emphasize their cultural identity, much like African-American youths who began to refer to themselves as black instead of Negro. Teatro Campesino's first performance was on the picket line of the grape strike in Delano. The play performed was "Las Dos Carnas del Patroncito," which dramatized the rejection of the assimilation of Mexican-American identity and the emergence of Chicano identity. Chávez's lack of interest in the Chicano Rights Movement, however, led to Teatro Campesino's disaffection. By 1968, it moved to the barrios of Los Angeles, where Chicano rights activities would soon boil over.

This inspiration for action did not come just from the fields of the San Joaquin Valley. More dramatically, the June 5, 1967, armed takeover of the county courthouse in San Amarilla, Arizona, by the Alianza Federal de Mercedes (Federal Alliance of Land Grants) got the attention of young Chicanos even more. Led by Reies López Tijerina, forty or more members of the Alianza took twenty hostages and demanded the return of lands—millions of acres in central and northern New Mexico—that had been stolen from the Hispano people (Spanish-Americans who were direct descendants of the original Spanish colonizers of New Mexico). Though the occupation lasted only one hour, a jailer and a state police officer were wounded in the melee. Afterward, Alianza participants fled into the mountains.

As was typical, the white-dominated state government overreacted and called out the National Guard to carry out a massive manhunt, complete with tanks. Dozens of innocent Hispanos—including women and children—were arrested and held for forty-eight hours, but more important, the action caught the attention of the entire nation. This was the first militant armed action by Mexican Americans anywhere in the Southwest for more than a hundred years. Though the Alianza was concerned only with the descendents of the original Spanish colonizers and not the general Mexican-American population, their demands resonated with all Latinos. The combination of Chávez's courage and perseverance in the face of overwhelming odds and the Alianza's armed occupation of the courthouse inspired young Chicanos to action.

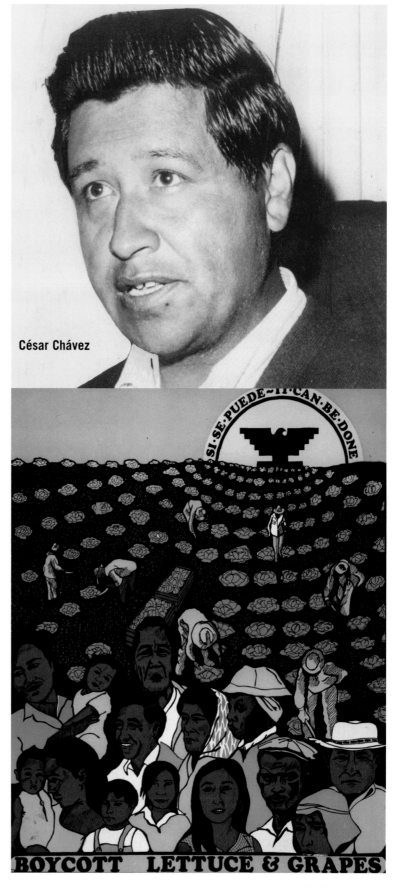

César Chávez

BOYCOTT LETTUCE & GRAPES

## "BLOW OUT!"

"BLOW OUT!"

That was the cry of more than a thousand students as they exited their classrooms together on the morning of March 3, 1968. The Abraham Lincoln High School in the heart of the East Los Angeles barrio was experiencing a strike. This was not a teacher's strike but a protest by the majority of Chicano students. Unlike many of the other student protests of the time, however, they were not acting on their own. Their march from the classrooms had been carefully planned with the help of one of the few Latino teachers in the school system, Sal Castro, as well as members of the community and the university student group UMAS.

The school grounds quickly crowded with protesters—students, activists, parents—shouting demands and waving placards reading CHICANO POWER!, VIVA LA RAZA (RACE)!, and VIVA LA REVOLUCIÓN! They handed out a sheet with thirty-six demands that had to be met before they returned to school. Their demands seem obvious in today's culture but were radical at the time. Among the issues were the end to racist school policies, the disciplining of racist teachers, the power of free speech, the inclusion of Mexican-American history and culture. Until then, the only history and culture taught in these predominantly Chicano schools was white

European culture. Any other music, literature, and history was denigrated and deemed not worthy of inclusion.

If the strike had been limited to Abraham Lincoln High School, perhaps nothing would have come of it. Within hours, though, more than 10,000 Chicano students had walked out of their classrooms. Word spread throughout the Los Angeles city school system, the largest in the nation, and Mexican-American students responded. By the end of the day, the entire system was brought to a standstill. For a week and a half the schools were shut down, and protesters marched in front of their schools, demanding not simply equal rights but respect for their heritage.

As the strike progressed, its importance extended well beyond its initial intentions of confronting school administrators or calling attention to the educational problems of Mexican-American youth. Instead, the strike was the first major mass protest explicitly against racism toward Mexican Americans in U.S. history. The "Blow Out" became not just a point of pride but the beginning of the Chicano Power Movement. Almost overnight, Chicano student activism on campuses and in schools increased dramatically.

The City of Los Angeles was not going to allow a few Mexican Americans to challenge their authority. Three months after the "Blow Out" and two days before

California's primary elections, thirteen young Mexican-American political activists were indicted by the Los Angeles County grand jury on conspiracy charges for their roles in organizing the strike. The indictments charged that the thirteen activists had conspired to "willfully disturb the peace and quiet" of the city of Los Angeles and disrupt the educational process in the schools. They were also branded as members of communist "subversive organizations" or outside agitators intent on radicalizing Mexican-American students. Each of the thirteen faced up to sixty-six years in prison if found guilty.

None of the thirteen were communists or members of "subversive organizations." They were, however, Mexican Americans who were very involved in their communities. They included:

- Sal Castro, the teacher who helped organize the walkout at Lincoln
- Eliezer Risco, the editor of a new community newspaper named *La Raza*
- Patricio Sanchez, a member of the university student organization MAPA
- Moctezuma Esparza, a member of UCLA UMAS
- David Sanchez, prime minister of the newly formed Brown Berets
- Carlos Montes, minister of communications of the Brown Berets
- Ralph Ramírez, minister of defense of the Brown Berets
- Fred Lopez, founding member of the Brown Berets
- Richard Vigil, community activist with the War on Poverty program
- Gilberto C. Olmeda, community activist with the War on Poverty program
- Joe Razo, community activist with the War on Poverty program
- Henry Gómez, community activist with the War on Poverty program
- Carlos Muñoz Jr., president of UMAS at California State College, Los Angeles

Rather than snuffing out the burgeoning Brown Power Movement, the indictments of the L.A. Thirteen ignited outrage among Mexican Americans. At the San José State College graduation, approximately 200 Chicano graduating seniors and members of the audience walked out in the middle of the commencement exercises. They said that they could not celebrate an institution that showed an utter lack of commitment to the Mexican-American community. They cited low enrollment of Mexican Americans at the college, inadequate training of professionals, teachers, social workers, police—who would go to work in their communities with no understanding of their culture—and an underlying racism at the college.

Throughout the following year, student strikes erupted at high schools across the Southwest. Most notably, in Denver, Colorado, and Crystal City, Texas, high school strikes led to broader concerns about Mexican-American rights. In Denver, the strike broke out into violent confrontations with the police. "Corky" Gonzáles took a leading role in the strike with his Crusade for Justice organization and enlisted many more members. Many students and activists were arrested, including Gonzáles.

This eventually led to the Crusade for Justice taking a leading role in the rapidly growing Chicano Power Movement. At the time, Gonzáles described what he

# This was not a teacher's strike but a protest by Chicano students.

wanted to do: "We are an awakening people, an emerging nation, a new breed." In March 1969, the Crusade organized a week-long National Chicano Youth Liberation Conference, in which it was stressed that Mexican Americans could not abandon their responsibility to their people for individualism and Americanization. The conference organizers called this Americanization the psychological "colonization" of Mexican-American youth. In response, they challenged Chicano youth to liberate themselves and suggested the way to do this was to find revolutionary models in their community. One place activists began looking was at street gangs and ex-convicts. Conference speakers proposed that henceforth, a crime committed by a Mexican American was a "revolutionary act."

**Aztlán:**
**a mythical origin**
**of the Aztecs**

The language and style of *vatos locos*, or gang members, became the social currency of student life. *Carnalismo* (the brotherhood code of Mexican-American youth gangs) would inform the nationalist ideology. This new Chicano identity was at the core of the rejection of white Anglo-Saxon Protestant culture and the embracing of *gabacho*—traditional Mexican—culture. By the end of the conference, participants had drafted a document called *El Plan Espiritual de Aztlán* (The Spiritual Plan of Aztlán). *El Plan* laid out a program to unite Mexican Americans. The preface to this manifesto read:

In the spirit of a new people that is conscious not only of its proud historical heritage, but also of the brutal "Gringo" invasion of our territories, we, the

Chicano inhabitants and civilizers of the northern land of Aztlán, from whence came our forefathers, reclaiming the land of their birth and consecrating the determination of our people of the sun, declare that the call of our blood is our power, or responsibility, and our inevitable destiny....We are Bronze People of a Bronze Culture....We are Aztlán.

A month after the Denver conference the Chicano Coordinating Council on Higher Education held a conference at the University of California, Santa Barbara. The goal of this conference was to find ways to implement *El Plan*. Out of the meeting came a new organization that brought together all the individual campus organizations, called El Movimiento Estudiantil Chicano de Aztlán (The Chicano Student Movement of Aztlán). This new group's acronym was MEChA, or "matchstick." Their intention was to light a fire in communities and on campuses to promote Chicano culture and rights. In a sense, these two conferences were a huge success. They brought together Chicanos from across the Southwest and West and united them in a single goal for the first time. Carlos Muñoz Jr., one of the original L.A. Thirteen and a participant in the conference, said:

The strategy called for students to be organized around social and cultural events that were designed to expose university indoctrination and propaganda based on the Protestant "ethic of profit and competition, of greed and intolerance." MEChA would advocate replacing that ethic with the values associated with the "ancestral communalism" of the ancient

# ANCESTRAL COMMUNALISM

**Mexican peoples. MEChA would appeal to the sense of obligation to family and community....**

In short, the Santa Barbara conference resolved to promote values, which were in direct opposition to America's mass market culture. In the conference attendees' minds, nothing short of this achievement would free them from American cultural colonization.

## THE CHICANO MORATORIUM

In the streets of the barrio, the Brown Berets became a tremendous influence. Taking their cue from the Black Panther Party, they were a paramilitary organization whose goal was to protect the community from police abuses. As in the Native-American and African-American communities, the police often used excessive force and brutality to enforce laws, some of which were on the books, some of which were not. The Brown Berets placed themselves as protectors of Chicano rights while authorities viewed them as terrorists and made a concerted effort to infiltrate and disrupt the Berets. What made the Berets different from MEChA was that its rank and file members

were primarily street youth, not students. Many of their members came from the ranks of *pintos*, those who had juvenile records. As such, they were also more representative of their working-class community, but were also eager to change the system. Student organizations fought for their rights within the system—at universities and within political organizations. The Brown Berets placed themselves in opposition to authority and promoted a goal of destruction of the system. From the perspective of those in power, this kind of direct threat had to be met with overwhelming force. Inevitably, this meant the two sides were destined for confrontation.

Finally, the explosion happened on August 29, 1970, in Los Angeles. Both MEChA and the Brown Berets had joined together to protest the Vietnam War with a demonstration called Chicano Moratorium. The Moratorium was the first major Mexican-American display of unity. Nearly 20,000 people gathered in East Los Angeles in Laguna Park to peacefully voice their resistance to the draft and the war. The police, however, quickly advanced on the demonstrators to break up the protest and ignited

Chicano Moratorium protest

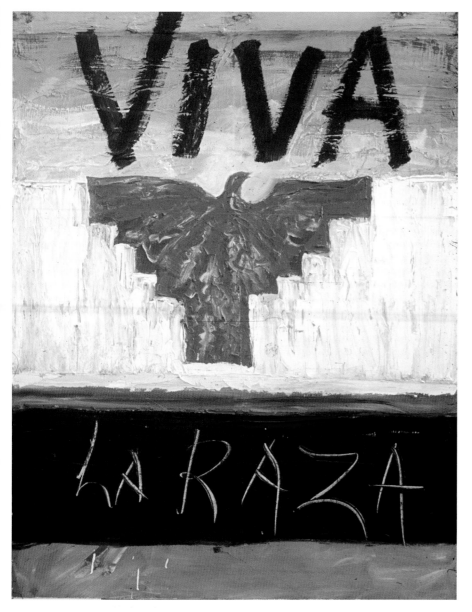

Painting created by Salvador Torres for a Chicano protest against the San Diego Gas and Electric Co. in 1969

Chicano Studies programs. As graduates students became part of the system they opposed, their investment in its destruction changed to a desire to expand its scope to include Chicano culture and Chicano Studies.

## LA RAZA UNIDA (THE UNITED RACE)

While California seemed to be the center of the Chicano Power Movement, Mexican Americans in other parts of the Southwest were also involved in promoting their rights and culture. Out of the school strike in Crystal City, Texas, arose a political party called El Partido de la Raza Unida (The Party of the United Race). For a couple of years Chicano activists had discussed the idea of a Mexican-American political party, but it had not gone much beyond talk. The Denver conference had concluded that there was a real need for the "creation of an independent, local, regional, and national political party" because neither the Republican nor the Democratic parties were concerned with Mexican-American needs.

a riot. Hundreds of participants were injured and three were killed. Many more were arrested, but not before the crowd turned into a mob. Along Whittier Boulevard in East Los Angeles, thousands of protesters expressed their outrage by burning businesses and cars. This seemed to shock not only the police but the demonstrators as well. Both sides seemed to retreat from their aggressive tactics, just as the same seemed to be happening all over the country. Mass demonstrations appeared to be at their end.

Later, as students began to graduate from their colleges, the student movement itself shifted its focus from the politics of confrontation to the implementation of

Two months after the Denver conference in May of 1969, organizers focused their attention on an area of south Texas called Winter Garden, which was more than 80 percent Mexican American. Their goal was to take control of the community institutions in this area through the political process. Their first target was the Crystal City school system. Crystal City was a community of approximately 10,000. Although the community was 80 percent Mexican, the power structure was white. In 1963, Mexican Americans, with the support of the Teamsters, were able to win seats on the city council, but that victory was short-lived. Two years later, they were voted off

"Mexican Americans...are reminding us all of the very powerful role of our personality, of the very wide extension of our cultural image and of the community action that is required if that identity is to become something more than a passing reference in celebrations."

—Mexican novelist Carlos Fuentes

because they had not developed a grassroots political organization to support them. White domination of the economy and overt racism made it impossible for Mexicans Americans to wrest control of the municipal government.

Despite the earlier failure at Crystal City, the strategy of La Raza Unida organizers was to begin with building the grassroots support first. Then they would attempt to gain control of city and county governments throughout south Texas. Their first step was again the Crystal City school system because the overwhelming Mexican-American population made it the most likely place to start. Their strategy to build support was to organize a student strike at the end of the year. Their goals were to promote support for education change by speaking to parents and families. La Raza Unida had instant success and gained control of both the school board and the city council. Party leader José Angel Gutiérrez summed up their aim:

**We sought to expose, confront, and eliminate the gringo. We felt it was necessary to polarize the community over issues into Chicano versus gringos.**

Despite Gutiérrez's confrontational language, La Raza Unida evolved into a party that sought to work within the political and economic structure of capitalism, unlike the Brown Berets. During a subsequent party convention in 1971, the Texas Unida Party crafted a platform that was decidedly not separatist or nationalist. The platform's four objectives were in fact quite mainstream:

1. Replace the existing system with a humanistic alternative which shall maintain equal representation of all people.
2. Create a government which serves the needs of individual communities, yet is beneficial to the general populace.
3. Create a political movement dedicated to ending the causes of poverty, misery, and injustice so that future generations can live a life free of exploitation.
4. Abolish racist practices within the existing social, educational, economic, and political system so that physical and cultural genocidal practices against minorities will be discontinued.

As the party spread throughout the Southwest and West, however, it became difficult to sustain the initial grassroots success. By 1973, the party went into decline. Like most third parties in the American political system, it was difficult to maintain over time. In addition to the winner-take-all nature of U.S. politics and the ability of the two major parties to co-opt the alternative party's issues, third parties find it almost impossible to succeed beyond one election cycle. La Raza Unida's success can best be measured in how much the Democratic and Republican parties have adopted not just Chicano issues  but broader policies that address concerns of different ethnic, racial, and religious backgrounds. In short, how much these parties have embraced pluralism can be traced back to the work done by groups like this.

# "They get one pat on the back here, and when they go outside they get ten slaps in the face."

**—Antonio Rodriguez, Principal, Bilingual Bicultural Art School, District 4, New York City**

## YOUNG LORDS
### Palante! Right on!

Shouts were followed by fists punching the air. Garbage cans trailing rotting trash arced high and smashed in the streets. It was the long, hot summer of 1969. Garbage had been left to decay in East Harlem, El Barrio, even though the sanitation department was nearby. They just weren't picking up. For weeks a group of youths calling themselves the New York City Young Lords Organization organized a street cleanup, but the city garbage trucks never came. Instead, the garbage rotted and a rank smell wafted across the neighborhood.

Eventually, the frustration boiled over, and the neighborhood, led by the Young Lords, began to drag the garbage into the middle of the street. They built a four-foot-high barrier on Third Avenue and shut down traffic. To ensure traffic remained stalled, they set the garbage on fire. Only then did the city respond, but they didn't send the sanitation department. They sent the NYPD and the fire department. Angry citizens met them with rocks, bottles, and trash.

The East Harlem Garbage Offensive became the unifying moment in New York's Puerto Rican population, and the moment when the Young Lords became the community's leading advocate. The New York City Young Lords Organization (later the Young Lords Party) was inspired by the Chicago gangs-turned-activists, the Young Lords Organization, and the Black Panther Party. Composed of mostly Puerto Rican students from SUNY-Old Westbury, Queens College, and Columbia Univer-

sity, many of its members had been involved in the student and anti-war movements. At first they formed "La Sociedad de Albizu Campos" in honor of Puerto Rican Nationalist Dr. Pedro Albizu Campos. This group was primarily a study group. When they decided action was necessary, they took on the Chicago gang's name and made it their mission to change the day-to-day conditions of the people in their community.

After massive migrations from Puerto Rico to the United States between 1948 and 1958, Puerto Ricans lived primarily in barrios in New York, Philadelphia, and Chicago. They had come to the States as people looking for decent jobs and housing, but found very little of either. Instead, they were pushed into manual labor and ghettos like East Harlem.

The Young Lords made it their project to change the lives of their families in concrete ways. After the garbage revolt, they went door-to-door and polled the community to find out what was important to them. In addition to cleaning streets, they developed a series of successful community projects, including breakfast and day care programs. In their desire to help their community, they targeted a local church as an ideal location in which to run many of their programs. The church, The First Spanish Methodist Church, was open only on Sundays and was unused the rest of the week. When the church elders refused to grant use to the Young Lords, the group commandeered the facility. They renamed the church La Iglesia de la Gente (The Church of the People) and turned it into a vibrant community center. They held the church for eleven days, during which more than 100,000 people came through the church's doors to participate in numerous community programs and events.

Out of this success, the Young Lords embarked on an even more ambitious project. They organized the Health Revolutionary Unity Movement, a mass organization made up of Puerto Rican and black medical workers based in Gouverneur Hospital on the Lower East Side and other hospitals in Harlem. HRUM did door-to-door TB testing and lead poisoning testing. They "liberated" a city TB-testing truck because it never came to Harlem, and they took chest X-rays of hundreds of people in the barrio.

After a young Puerto Rican woman died from minor surgery, HRUM took over the old Lincoln Hospital on November 10, 1970. Over 600 people joined in occupying the Nurses' Residence to publicize flagrant disregard for human life in New York hospitals. The occupation was brief, but was supported by most of the hospital staff, and embarrassed the city tremendously.

Like the Black Panther Party, the Brown Berets, and AIM, the Young Lords quickly gained the attention of the FBI and their COINTELPRO. Agents of the FBI began to infiltrate the Young Lords and disrupt them. When the group was hit by the FBI and NYPD, one of those arrested, Julio Roldan, purportedly committed suicide that night in jail. The suicide was clearly suspicious, since Roldan was an active and vital member of the Young Lords and had anticipated his arrest. In response, the group occupied the People's Church a second time. This time, however, they

were armed. With this action the Young Lords became radicalized in a way that they had never been previously. Their concrete community solutions began to be replaced with extremist ideological stances. They quoted from Mao's *Little Red Book* and required all members to be ideologically pure in support of Marx, Lenin, and Mao. By 1971, they had marginalized themselves by beginning the self-destructive process of weeding out anyone who doubted the scientific truth of these leaders.

"For the first time in the history of the world, every human being is now subjected to contact with dangerous chemicals, from the moment of conception to death. In less than two decades of their use, the synthetic pesticides have been so thoroughly distributed throughout the animate and inanimate world that they occur virtually everywhere."

—Rachel Carson, *Silent Spring*

EARTH DAY

# THE ORIGINS OF THE ENVIRONMENTAL MOVEMENT

## ELIXIRS OF DEATH

We are poisoning ourselves, and everything we touch. That was the frightening message Rachel Carson voiced in her groundbreaking article in *The New Yorker* magazine and then in her bestselling book *Silent Spring* in 1962. Writing the book while she was dying of cancer, perhaps poisoned by the very world she was writing about, Carson redefined the way Americans thought about their environment. She explained how humankind's relationship with nature was an "intricate web of life whose interwoven strands lead from microbes to man."

For the first time, someone was offering a devastating critique of the chemical industry. She revealed the effects that indiscriminate use of inorganic chemicals, such as DDT, had on the world's ecological system. After World War II, the new and amazing pesticides, herbicides, and fungicides that industry produced seemed like miracles. According to their producers, they "controlled" all kinds of pesky insects, fungi, and weeds. What no one really understood until Carson put all the pieces together was that these new wonder chemicals were also poisoning us and our environment. Her research, supported with more than fifty-five pages of references in the back of her book, exposed cancer-inducing chemicals that remained as residues in virtually everything we ate or drank.

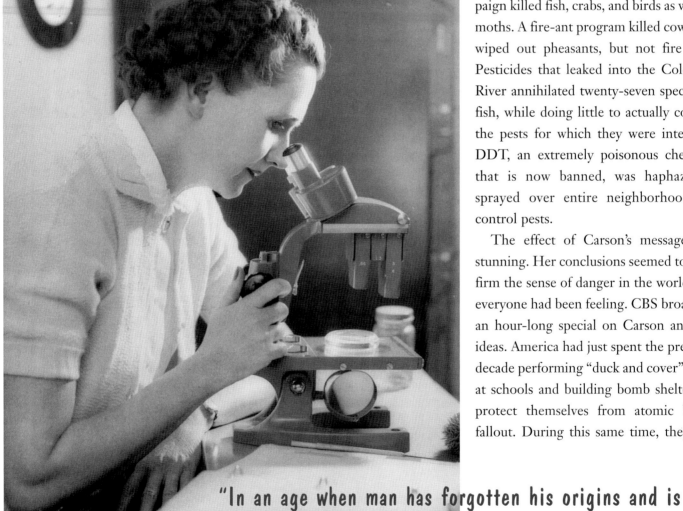

The book catalogued the many instances where pesticide spraying caused irreparable damage to the entire environment. A gypsy-moth eradication campaign killed fish, crabs, and birds as well as moths. A fire-ant program killed cows and wiped out pheasants, but not fire ants. Pesticides that leaked into the Colorado River annihilated twenty-seven species of fish, while doing little to actually control the pests for which they were intended. DDT, an extremely poisonous chemical that is now banned, was haphazardly sprayed over entire neighborhoods to control pests.

The effect of Carson's message was stunning. Her conclusions seemed to confirm the sense of danger in the world that everyone had been feeling. CBS broadcast an hour-long special on Carson and her ideas. America had just spent the previous decade performing "duck and cover" drills at schools and building bomb shelters to protect themselves from atomic bomb fallout. During this same time, they had

"In an age when man has forgotten his origins and is blind even to his most essential needs of survival, water has become the victim of his indifference." —Rachel Carson

# We have met the enemy, and he is us.

**—This popular saying appeared on posters and bumper stickers.**

spent their leisure time watching Godzilla and other mutant creatures wreaking havoc in movie theaters. The notion that an even more insidious contamination might really exist seemed highly implausible.

Suddenly, progress and prosperity had a dark and destructive underside. Not everything industry produced was good for you—some of it in fact was deadly. That marvelous green blanket of grass spreading so uniformly across your yard required pesticides and fertilizers that were poisoning the environment. America's great icon, the bald eagle, was in danger of extinction because of DDT.

Of all our natural resources water has become the most precious. By far the greater part of the earth's surface is covered by its enveloping seas, yet in the midst of this plenty we are in want. By a strange paradox, most of the earth's abundant water is not usable for agriculture, industry, or human consumption because of its heavy load of sea salts, and so most of the world's population is either experiencing or is threatened with critical shortages. In an age when man has forgotten his origins and is blind even to his most essential needs of survival, water along with other resources has become the victim of his indifference.

The problem of water pollution by pesticides can be understood in the context, as part of the whole it belongs to—the pollution of the total environment of mankind. The pollution entering our waterways comes from many sources: radioactive wastes from reactors, laboratories, and hospitals; fallout from nuclear explosions; domestic wastes from cities and towns; chemical wastes from factories. To these wastes is added a new kind of fallout—the chemical sprays applied to croplands and gardens, forests and fields. Many of these chemical agents in this alarming mélange imitate and augment the harmful effects of radiation, and within the groups of chemicals themselves there are sinister and little-understood interaction, transformations, and summations of effect.

## SAVE THE BAY

Because Carson's *Silent Spring* was a national best-seller, her message reached some surprising places. Some of the first people to realize that Carson's message contained hard truths were hunters and fishermen. Over the years, they'd watched as their lakes and rivers became polluted with improperly treated sewage and industrial waste. They were catching fish with odd growths and mutations. They were experiencing a wildlife population crash. What was unusual about them, however, was that most of them were not traditional activists. Instead they were professionals and business owners, and they had political and community clout. They weren't the radical youths who were burning their draft cards and dropping acid. They were part of the establishment and were used to being listened to.

One of the earliest of these groups emerged right in the shadow of the country's political power center, Washington, D.C. Because of its proximity, the Chesapeake Bay was a highly visible natural resource, but the impact of pollution was having a destructive toll. In 1966, a group of Baltimore businessmen who enjoyed sailing, hunting, and fishing on and around the Chesapeake Bay recognized the problem and mobilized. They met with their congressman, Rogers C. B. Morton, to express their concerns about the bay. From their perspective, the future of the bay looked grim. They could envision only more boats, more people, more houses, poor sewage treatment, and dirty industrial discharges, all of which threatened the ecological balance. If things continued as they had been moving, the environment, which had thrived with all kinds of fish, waterfowl, and flora, would become a desolate landfill.

Morton felt his options were limited without pressure on Congress from the private sector. He suggested the group form a "private-sector organization that can represent the best interests of the Chesapeake Bay. It should

Club made the wilderness a quality-of-life issue rather than a resource to harness for progress. They promoted nature as a retreat from the modern world where one could find spiritual seclusion and meditation. This strategy transformed wilderness preservation from simply a conservation issue to a moral one. The Sierra Club was central in the passage of the 1964 Wilderness Act and stopping the Bureau of Reclamation from building two dams on the Colorado River in the Grand Canyon National Park.

The CBF extended this approach by not simply focusing on preservation but emphasizing restoration of damaged or

Cuyahoga River fire

build public concern, then encourage government and private citizens to deal with these problems together." Led by Arthur Sherwood, the group chartered the Chesapeake Bay Foundation (CBF) in 1967 to advocate for the bay.

The CBF took its cue from the Sierra Club, which had already transformed itself into an activist and reform-oriented lobbying group. The club led the way in the early sixties by redefining the country's relationship with its natural resources. Through full-page ads in papers, letter-writing campaigns, and grassroots organizing, the Sierra

destroyed ecosystems. They group recruited committed conservationists, but also anyone who had an interest in the Chesapeake watershed. Beginning with a campaign of environmental education, CBF adopted "Save the Bay" as its motto and distributed thousands of blue-and-white bumper stickers. Then the foundation embarked on an ambitious lobbying campaign of resource protection that promoted control and regulation of the watershed.

Like the Population Crisis Committee and the Environmental Defense Fund, both of which also formed

## ENVIRONMENTAL DISASTERS THAT SHOOK THE NATION

In March of 1967, the *Torrey Canyon* oil tanker spilled 117,000 tons of crude oil into the English Channel.

In February of 1969, off the coast of Santa Barbara, California, an oil rig spilled millions of gallons of crude oil that washed up onto the beaches of appalled and normally privileged homeowners.

On June 22, 1969, the heavily polluted Cuyahoga River caught fire. Pollutants also fueled fires on a river into the Baltimore Harbor, on the Buffalo River in upstate New York, and on the Rouge River in Michigan. Despite the fact that the Cuyahoga wasn't the only body of water to catch fire that year, it was this fire that seemed emblematic and spurred the government to enact the Clean Water Act. Congressman Louis Stokes commented, "The Cuyahoga will live in infamy as the only river that was ever declared a fire hazard."

In 1969, Lake Erie was declared endangered by chemical and sewage pollution.

around this time, the CBF emphasized the interrelation between human and environmental concerns. They crafted a message that progress could not be sustained unless we protected our resources. In this way, environmentalism shifted from a nostalgia for a past wilderness to a more scientific examination of our interdependency.

# the movement had become my enemy

## BACK TO THE LAND

Good morning, Henry Thoreau, good morning me, good morning you. Good morning, good morning, good morning. In my dim recall of yesterday, the beaver pond rose till we stood apart and alone on the planet. Silent's boat shoved off on the waters and we wondered who among all those millions would make it with us to dawn. Mark has been making a creakity wooden sign saying "Total Loss Farm" so they'll know the place when they get here. My arms and legs and kidneys and heart are yet moving. I am yet carrying myself outside to look to the east and sign to the sun. Good morning, good morning, good morning.

Between 1967 and 1969, more than 137 environment-related bills were introduced before Congress.

For Raymond Mungo, author of *Total Loss Farm*, it was a new morning. Like his peers, he was worn out from the violent demonstrations in cities and on college campuses. For nearly a million other youths, the notion of returning to something simple and more authentic than atomic bombs and modern industrialization was a real draw. *Total Loss Farm* tracked a year on a Vermont commune. First published in the *Atlantic Monthly*, it was nominated for a Pulitzer Prize. The book recounts Mungo's and his friends' attempt to create a utopian community that would be sustainable. These new homesteaders believed that a return to nature would lead them to their true selves. The memoir marked a coming of age for an idea that had been gaining momentum since the mid-'60s, the Back-to-the-Land Movement.

Inspired by Thomas Jefferson's agrarian vision and Henry David Thoreau's retreat to Walden Pond, the Back-to-the-Land Movement sprang up as a counter to everything its proponents despised. Disillusioned by their lack of ability to change American culture, these youths decided to retreat to communities of their own making. The Movement's main purpose was to resurrect an agrarian way of life and to live within a self-imposed set of guidelines that rejected mainstream American culture. The proponents' lives were meant to challenge consumerism, violence, greed, and exploitation of the environment.

In their effort to begin anew, these groups turned away from an ownership society and created a communal one. Property ownership, child care, food production, and decision-making were all done together. No one person was supposed to be in charge. Mungo describes this idyllic world and the dreams he felt were possible:

"They do not yet realize that their heirs will refuse to inhabit their hollow cities...."

It was the farm that had allowed me the luxury of this vision, for the farm had given me insulation from America which the peace movement promised but cruelly denied. When we lived in Boston, Chicago, San Francisco, Washington. . . we dreamed of a New Age born of violent insurrection. We danced on the graves of war dead in Vietnam, every corpse was ammunition for Our Side; we set up a counter government down there in Washington, had marches, rallies and meetings; tried to fight fire with fire. Then Johnson resigned, yes, and the universities began to fall, the best and oldest ones first, and by God every 13-year-old in the suburbs was smoking dope and our numbers multiplied into the millions. But I woke up in the spring of 1968 and said, "This is not what I had in mind," because the movement had become my enemy; the movement was not flowers and doves and spontaneity, but another vicious system, the seed of a heartless bureaucracy, a minority Party vying for power rather than peace. It was then that we put away the schedule for the revolution, gathered together our dear ones and all our resources, and set off to Vermont in search of the New Age.

The New Age we were looking for proved to be very old indeed, and I've often wondered aloud at my luck for being 23 years old in a time and place in which only the past offers hope and inspiration; the future offers only artifice and blight. I travel now in a society of friends who heat their homes with hand-cut wood and eliminate in outhouses, who cut pine shingles with draw-knives and haul maple sugar sap on sleds, who weed potatoes with their university-trained hands, pushing long hair out of their way and thus marking their foreheads with beautiful penitent dust. We till the soil to atone for our fathers' destruction of it. We smell. We live far from the marketplaces in America by our own volition, and the powerful men left behind are happy to have us out of their way. They do not yet realize that their heirs will refuse to inhabit their hollow cities, will find them poisonous and lethal, will run back to the Stone Age if necessary for survival and peace.

The commune was another image that defined this era. Long-haired, long-skirted hippies living together in seeming harmony—sharing food production, child-rearing, creating egalitarian communities. The hard work, not to mention the very real compromise that it took to sustain these communities, may not have lasted, but many of the practices begun in those small utopias remain popular today. Organic farming, food cooperatives, holistic medicine and lifestyles, herbal medicines, recycling—all these ideas have long outlasted their alternative beginnings.

## EARTH DAY

That big blue marble, our Earth, which suddenly appeared on the nation's television screen on July 20, 1969, seemed to be floating alone in the darkness of space. For the first time, it was as if the entire world were looking in a mirror at itself. In reality, the image came from a camera pointed at the Earth by the astronauts of the *Apollo XI* moon mission 252,000 miles away. Suddenly, the entire nation was united in awe at the miracle of Earth.

Nine months later, on April 22, 1970, that wonder translated into one of the most notable events in our nation's history: Earth Day. The biggest symbol of the rise in awareness and power of the environmental movement was the establishment of Earth Day on April 22, 1970. *American Heritage Magazine* called the event "one of the most remarkable happenings in the history of democracy…20 million people demonstrated their support…American politics and public policy would never be the same again."

The idea for Earth Day began more than seven years earlier when Senator Gaylord Nelson of Wisconsin came to the decision to find a way to put environmental issues into the forefront of everyone's mind. Initially, he convinced President Kennedy to go on a five-day, eleven-state conservation tour in September 1963, but the presidential bully pulpit did not succeed in putting the environment on the national agenda. For Nelson, however, this was only a beginning.

"I continued to speak on environment issues to a variety of audiences in some twenty-five states," wrote Nelson. "All across the nation, evidence of environmental degradation was appearing everywhere, and everyone noticed but the political establishment." Nelson knew that he had time on his side. The environment was only going to get worse. He just needed to continue the pressure. Years later, Nelson described the process of how Earth Day evolved:

Six years would pass before the idea that became Earth Day occurred to me while on a conservation speaking tour out West in the summer of 1969. At that time, the anti-Vietnam War demonstrations, called "teach-ins," had spread to college campuses all across the nation. Suddenly, the idea occurred to me—why not organize a huge grassroots protest over what was happening to our environment?

I was satisfied that if we could tap into the environmental concerns of the general public and infuse the student anti-war energy into the environmental cause, we could generate a demonstration that would force the issue onto the political agenda….

At a conference in Seattle in September 1969, I announced that in the spring of 1970 there would be a nationwide grassroots demonstration on behalf of the environment and invited everyone to participate. The wire services carried the story coast to coast. The response was electric….Telegrams, letters, and telephone inquiries poured in from all across the country. The American people finally had a forum to express their concern about what was happening to the land, rivers, lakes, and air—and they did so with spectacular exuberance. For the next four months, two members of my Senate staff, Linda Billings and John Heritage, managed Earth Day affairs out of my Senate office….

Earth Day worked because of the spon-

Pollution: it's a crying shame

People start pollution.
People can stop it.
Keep America Beautiful

**taneous response at the grassroots level.**
We had neither the time nor resources to organize 20
million demonstrators and the thousands of schools
and local communities that participated. That was the
remarkable thing about Earth Day. It organized itself.

Ten million children participated in planting thousands
of trees in commemoration of the event. Schools organized special Earth Day fairs and assemblies. More than
100,000 people demonstrated at the Washington
Monument in Washington, D.C. All across the country, at
various landmarks, speakers described the destruction of
the environment by reckless industries and expressed
hope that we as members of the human race could work

together to preserve the earth's continued health.

Earth Day created an overwhelming momentum in
Washington, D.C. Republicans and Democrats were united
on this issue. The result was the creation of the
Environmental Protection Agency and the Occupational
Safety and Health Act. A host of new regulations, cleanup
programs, and technological solutions were suddenly proposed. Clearly, ecology was an issue on which all of America
could unite. It contained none of the divisive issues such as
poverty, race, and war. It transcended race riots, assassina-
tions, and generational conflicts. With extensive support,
the government could enact a wide range of legislation to
limit corporate pollution and manage the country's natural
resources. By 1972, even DDT was outlawed by Congress.

"To me all the problems began in the Sixties."

—retired Texas Republican Congressman and House Majority Leader Dick Armey

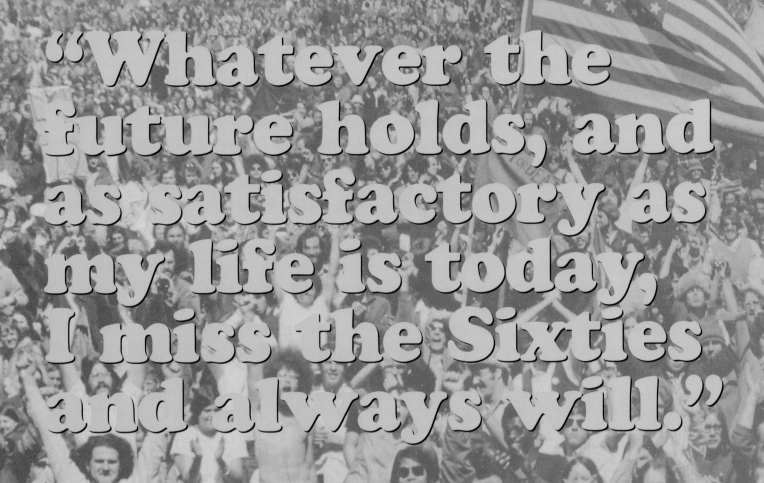

"Whatever the future holds, and as satisfactory as my life is today, I miss the Sixties and always will."

—former Democratic State Senator in California, former SDS activist and Chicago Seven defendant Tom Hayden

A more equitable nation

# MAKING A RAINBOW

or the rise of a welfare state?

When it comes to the '6os, everyone seems to disagree. Armey and Hayden are not unique in their completely opposite assessments of the era. No two people seem to be able to agree on the legacy of the '6os. Some saw a more equitable and humane nation, open to all its citizens. Others decried the rise of the welfare state, where the government intervened to take away personal responsibility.

Passionate reactions confirm just how important and influential the era was. Whether or not you believe this decade had a positive influence on contemporary culture, it has affected us all—even those who were born a decade or more later. Every aspect of the nation changed, from the highest levels of government and corporate culture to how we dispose of our garbage.

Just a quick glance around your neighborhood will provide real evidence.

In almost every village, town, and city in the country, people set aside their used plastic, glass jars, aluminum, metal, and newspapers. Then, once a week, these items are either set curbside in blue containers to be collected or dropped off at waste management centers for recycling. As well, a significant portion of the American populace compost kitchen and yard wastes in their backyards. Before the '6os all of that trash would have been buried in the town dump in such a way that it would not decompose for a millennium or more. That town and city dumps are now called waste management centers tells us a lot about how our thinking has changed about the environment.

On the streets today, many of the cars are hybrids that contain engines running on a combination of batteries and gasoline. These cars emit significantly less pollution than traditional gasoline-fueled vehicles and have become the fastest-growing segment in the automotive industry. But the passage of the clean air and water acts in Congress are still threatened by companies opting out of the compliance and by developers drilling in protected areas.

On a national level, minorities have gained significant representation, influence, and power in government. Perhaps the most dramatic example is in Memphis, Tennessee, the city where Martin Luther King Jr. was assassinated. Memphis now has an African-American mayor, an African-American U.S. congressman, and a predominantly African-American city council. When King died, the government establishment was all white, despite the fact that nearly half of the city's citizens were black. Birmingham, Alabama, nicknamed Bombingham in the '6os for all the racial bombings, is also governed by an African-American mayor. This change in the power structure of local governments is common all over the South as well as in other parts of the country.

## SUSTAINABILITY

In the late 1990s a new approach to thinking about humankind's relationship with the environment was captured in the coining of the term "Sustainability." Though the word has been around for centuries, only recently has it become popular to use to describe an attempt to provide the best outcomes for the human and natural environments both now and into the future. Sustainability describes the attempt to coordinate economic, social, institutional, and environmental areas to protect and nourish both the human and nonhuman environment.

Despite this real progress, not all African Americans have found a route to the American Dream. Although blacks account for only 12 percent of the U.S. population, 44 percent of all prisoners in the United States are black. About a third of all African-American men are under the supervision of the criminal justice system, and about 12 percent of African-American men in their twenties and

| RISING MEDIAN AGE | | |
|---|---|---|
| **27** | **33.3** | **35.3** |
| 1970 | 1990 | 2000 |

| U.S. POPULATION | **1945** | **1995** |
|---|---|---|
| Life expectancy | 65.9 | 75.7 |
| High school graduates | 25% | 81% |
| College graduates | 5% | 22% |

## BROWN IS BEAUTIFUL—AND THE MAJORITY BY 2050

By 2050, the non-Hispanic White population of the United States will drop below 50 percent. This means that brown will become the dominant color in America. People of African, Middle Eastern, Asian, and Hispanic descent will make up the majority of Americans.

| Population | **2000** | **2050** |
|---|---|---|
| White | 195.7 million | 210.3 million |
| Hispanic | 35.6 | 102.6 |
| Asian | 10.7 | 33.4 |
| Black | 35.8 | 61.4 |

thirties are incarcerated. These astronomical incarceration rates have huge social and economic consequences for black women, black children, and black communities.

Still, race, ethnicity, and gender have on the whole become less of a factor in the public sphere. Despite the fact that women and minorities have not yet won the highest office in the nation—the presidency—they are represented on the Supreme Court and as heads of key federal departments, such as secretary of state and attorney general. One encouraging indication of how the country's views on race have changed is Nike's "Be Like Mike" advertising campaign in the 1990s. Considered the greatest basketball player ever, Michael Jordan so inspired kids and adults that he transcended racial boundaries to become America's iconic hero. Before the '60s this would never have happened.

For women, changes begun in the '60s have meant a steady movement toward equality in the workplace and at home. Though women's salaries are still not comparable to men's, they have increased steadily. In 1963, women earned 58 cents for every dollar a man made. Today, that has risen to 76 cents to every dollar a man makes. Corporations have changed their policies to allow women maternity leave, which was not the case before the Women's Liberation Movement. This openness to women's issues has also made it possible for men to get paternity leave. It has encouraged corporations to offer its employees on-site day care and leave for elder care. None of this would have happened without women speaking up for their rights. Though women still struggle with balancing career goals and motherhood, the real difference from the '60s is that women are in this struggle, instead of in the battle to be allowed to have a job at all.

The most visible area of improvement for women has been in sports. With the 1972 enactment of Title IX by the U.S. government—which guarantees equal access to sports for women—women's participation in sports has skyrocketed from 290,000 high school girls to more than

1.9 million high school girls participating in competitive sports. The benefits of Title IX also surface in other areas of women's lives. High school girls who participate in competitive sports are less likely to become pregnant while in school and are more likely to graduate from high school. The downside of increased participation by women has been that men's sports programs at high schools and colleges now have to compete for the same dollars. This has led some schools to eliminate expensive sports programs such as football in order to balance the needs of women's programs.

For Native Americans, the most obvious difference has been the fact that the U.S. government has changed its policy of trying to eliminate their culture. Now Indian tribes have a lot more freedom not just to celebrate and practice their cultural heritage but also to make their own choices about their lives. One of the biggest indicators of this change is the increase of people who claim Native American heritage. In 1960, only 524,000 people identified themselves as American Indian. By 1990, that number had risen to 1.9 million, and by 2000, the number more than doubled to 4.1 million. That's nearly an 800 percent increase.

Many tribes across the country have established profitable casinos, which have raised the living conditions of its members. Consequently, the median household income of Native Americans ($31,799) has risen above that of African Americans ($28,679) and Hispanics ($31,703). This is a significant change for the positive when you consider that Native Americans were the poorest minority in the country and were subject to a government policy of annihilation. The sad fact, however, is that American Indians, like most other minorities in the United States, still lag behind the dominant white culture when it comes to economic success and opportunity.

When looking at the progress Hispanics have made in America, one number stands out: Between 2000 and 2050, the Hispanic population is expected to triple, from 35.6

## NOTABLE BOOMERS

**Bill Clinton** (B. 1946) PRESIDENT

**George W. Bush** (B. 1946) PRESIDENT

**Steven Spielberg** (B. 1946) FILMMAKER

**David Letterman** (B. 1947) LATE-NIGHT TV HOST

**Rush Limbaugh** (B. 1951) RIGHT-WING RADIO COMMENTATOR

**Oprah Winfrey** (B. 1954) TV HOST AND PRODUCER

**Howard Stern** (B. 1954) RADIO "SHOCK JOCK"

**Denzel Washington** (B. 1954) ACTOR

**Bill Gates** (B. 1955) MICROSOFT FOUNDER, WEALTHIEST PERSON IN AMERICA

**Steve Jobs** (B. 1955) COFOUNDER, APPLE AND PIXAR

**Spike Lee** (B. 1957) FILMMAKER

million to 102.6 million. The voice and power of Americans of Hispanic origin are increasing. California is home to 12.4 million Hispanics, while Texas is home to 7.8 million. Thirteen states—including Arizona, New York, Georgia, Illinois, and Washington—have Hispanic populations of more than half a million. Bill Richardson, the governor of New Mexico, is Hispanic. One characteristic that describes Hispanic culture and heritage is diversity. Hispanic people come from all over South America, Central America, the Caribbean, and Mexico. What binds them is that they can

# WHO SAYS
# Too Much Freedom Is Too Much?

Nearly every night gay bars and clubs were raided in cities across America. Gays and lesbians were harassed, beaten and arrested simply because of their sexual orientation in the '60s. In the early morning of June 28, 1969, around 1:30 a.m., the gay community had finally had enough. Police raided an illegal bar, the Stonewall Inn, in Greenwich Village. Rather than simply run, like most patrons did when police raided a gay bar, customers resisted. Within minutes the police were overwhelmed. More than 2,000 people chanted "Gay Power!" and threw bottles and rocks at the police. Over the next few days gays and lesbians battled the police. Hundreds were beaten and injured. The Stonewall Riot became the signature event that launched the gay rights movement and began the long, difficult fight to change public opinion on homosexuality.

In 1965, 82 percent of men and 52 percent of women said that homosexuality represented a "clear threat" to the American way of life. By 2005, a CBS poll recorded just how much opinions had changed over forty years. Fifty-seven percent of Americans now believed that homosexuals should be allowed to enter into either marriage or civil union relationships. Another 2005 poll, this time by Gallup, showed that 90 percent of the respondents believed that gays and lesbians deserved protections against employment discrimination. Unfortunately, only seventeen states and the District of Columbia ban discrimination based on sexual orientation, while only eight states ban discrimination based on gender orientation. The gay rights movement has made extraordinary advances since Stonewall in 1969, but LBGT (Lesbian, Bisexual, Gay, and Transgender) people are the victims every day of small and large discriminations that go unnoticed by the rest of the country's population.

Protesters outside the Stonewall Bar in New York City, the location of the first gay and lesbian demonstration in 1969

# The era of the Sixties exposed many fault lines in our culture and gave voice to many who had none previously.

trace their origin or descent to Spain. While Hispanics are making considerable progress, they still trail behind their non-Hispanic White counterparts in income, jobs, education, and housing. The hope is that as the country becomes more brown and less white, more and more opportunities will open up. Only time will tell.

The legacy is that overt discrimination and government-sanctioned discrimination against minorites has been outlawed. There are now laws in place that guarantee many of the rights and liberties that were limited during the '60s. Where progress most noticeably has lagged has been with economic opportunity. Sociologist Eric J. Krieg argues that "racism is built into the very structure of our economic system." In short, while our laws prohibit racism, our economic system of unfettered capitalism still leaves those without money vulnerable. He sees this vulnerability manifest itself in neighborhoods of the economically weak—those who live in low-income communities and communities of color. These neighborhoods are most likely also to be the home of the most dangerous hazardous waste sites. As an example, he cites the HUD public housing in North Cambridge, Massachusetts. "These enormous towers and open spaces with soccer fields were built on top of a landfill," explains Krieg. "Here you have a great economic decision, saving state money by placing people in need of housing right-square in the middle of the most polluted section of town." When Krieg sees figures of high rates of childhood leukemia and asthma as well as low scores in local schools, he's not surprised. "If you live in a poisonous environment, that home is going to be a contributing factor in the causes of bad health and education," he concludes. It's basic logic, when common sense tells us our home is our castle—or perhaps our grave.

Another highly controversial issue to come out of the '60s was the emergence of women's reproductive rights. Birth control pills allowed women to be in charge of their bodies in ways that were inconceivable to the previous generation. Women could choose whether to become pregnant or not. This allowed women to go to college and start careers. Although the landmark abortion case *Roe v. Wade* did not occur until 1973, it was clearly a legacy of the women's rights movement. The Supreme Court's granting women the right to choose whether or not to terminate a pregnancy in the first trimester is an enduring controversy that still divides this nation.

Most people witnessed the dramatic disparity between the affluent and the poor in 2005, when Hurricane Katrina hit New Orleans. The poor communities in New Orleans, which were predominantly African American, suffered the most. These neighborhoods were largely located in the most vulnerable areas below sea level. Unlike more affluent communities, which were on higher ground, these areas were most at risk of flooding and also least able to protect themselves. It was also these poor communities that were not evacuated, because the city did not provide transportation to those who did not have their own cars and trucks. What Hurricane Katrina highlighted was a vulnerability that poor communities have because they are not affluent. Because they are poor and lack economic power, they do not have strong representation in the business community or in government.

The era of the '60s exposed many fault lines in our culture and gave voice to many who had none previously. That some of the issues raised and some of the revolutions started are still ongoing demonstrates how deep seated these problems are and how necessary it is that our democracy continue to debate them. The lesson learned from the '60s was that all people—young, old, and in between—could make a difference. In the decade that came before our bicentennial celebration in 1976, that was an important lesson indeed.

## 1946

Bob Hope, Bing Crosby, and Dorothy Lamour open in the film *Road to Utopia*.

First U.S.-built rocket leaves Earth's atmosphere and reaches 50-mile height.

Ho Chi Minh elected president of Democratic Republic of Vietnam.

Chou En-lai, communist liaison to nationalists, declares all-out war for control of China.

U.S. detonates fourth atom bomb in test off Bikini Atoll.

Joe McCarthy defeats Robert La Follette for Senate seat in Wisconsin.

The number of births in the United States is 3,411,000, an increase of nearly 600,000 from 1945 and the highest number recorded in the nation's history so far.

## 1947

Kareem Abdul-Jabbar, Hall of Fame NBA player, is born.

Gen. Marshall, commander of European reconstruction, says moving toward a unified Europe is a condition for U.S. aid.

Mexican-American veterans organize the American G.I. Forum in response to a Three Rivers, Texas, funeral home's denial to bury a Mexican-American soldier killed during World War II.

World Bank grants Dutch $195 million reconstruction loan.

Harry S Truman committee proposes $17 billion European recovery plan.

Tennessee Williams's play *A Streetcar Named Desire* opens on Broadway in New York. The play is directed by Elia Kazan and stars Marlon Brando.

## 1948

Truman proposes free two-year community colleges for all who want an education.

U.S. Supreme Court rules religious instruction in public school's unconstitutional.

Truman signs foreign assistance act.

U.S. Supreme Court bans pacts barring African Americans from owning real estate.

World's biggest telescope, at 200 inches in diameter, is dedicated at Mount Palomar, California.

Chuck Yeager exceeds the speed of sound in a Bell XS-1 jet.

Chinese radio announces formation of communist North China People's Government.

Truman assails HUAC as more un-American than the people it investigates.

HUAC implicates film star Charlie Chaplin as a communist sympathizer.

New York's Metropolitan Opera televised for the first time with *Othello*.

## 1949

Berlin airlift delivers one million tons of cargo to West Berliners cut off from the West by communist East Germany.

Dean Martin and Jerry Lewis complete first film together, *My Friend Irma*.

Berlin blockade is ended.

Communist forces sweep through China.

Truman says nation hysterical over Reds, or communists.

Actress Meryl Streep is born.

RCA announces invention of system for broadcasting color television.

The Soviet Union explodes its first atomic bomb.

Harvard Law School begins admitting women for the first time.

China establishes the People's Republic of China and hails new leader Mao Tse-tung.

HUAC chairman Parnell Thomas is sentenced to six to eighteen months for padding congressional payrolls.

## 1950

U.S. Senate adopts the Equal Rights Amendment to the Constitution by a 63–14 vote.

McCarthy launches anti-Red campaign.

Children spend almost as much time watching TV, 27 hours a week, as they do attending school.

North Korea invades South.

Supreme Court bars segregation in two colleges.

U.S. forces see action in South Korea for the first time.

U.S. population is recorded at 150,520,198—nearly 19 million more than in 1940.

The U.S. government publishes a 438-page guide on civilian defense against atomic bomb attacks.

Emigration from Mexico doubles from 5.9 percent to 11.9 percent of the total number of immigrants to the United States.

## 1951

Julius and Ethel Rosenberg are found guilty of spying for the Soviet Union and are sentenced to death.

United States tests hydrogen bomb.

Television broadcasts its first human birth.

Bikini outfits are banned from Wimbledon Tennis Championships.

J. D. Salinger's *The Catcher in the Rye* is published.

Average yearly income for an American reaches $1,436.

A truce line drawn roughly along the 38th parallel divides North and South Korea.

## 1952

King George VI of England dies. Queen Elizabeth II is coronated.

Three-color traffic lights adopted by New York.

Gene Kelly stars in *Singin' in the Rain*.

Nevada A-bomb blast televised.

TWA begins first "tourist class" airline service, landing 95 passengers in Shannon, Ireland.

*Anne Frank: The Diary of a Young Girl* published in U.S.

New York City dismisses eight teachers for alleged communist activities.

Harvard's Paul Zoll becomes the first to use electric shock to treat cardiac arrest.

Eisenhower wins presidential election in a landslide.

John F. Kennedy wins Massachusetts Senate seat.

Ralph Ellison's *Invisible Man* is published.

George Jorgenson has a sex operation to change into Christine Jorgenson, a woman.

## 1953

Walt Disney's *Peter Pan* premieres.

Dr. Jonas Salk develops a successful vaccine for polio.

Thirty-fifth nuclear blast test occurs in Nevada.

Jacqueline Cochran becomes the first woman to break the sound barrier.

Ernest Hemingway wins the Pulitzer Prize for his novel *The Old Man and the Sea*.

Frank Sinatra wins a best supporting actor Oscar for his role in *From Here to Eternity*.

Earl Warren chosen as U.S. chief justice of the Supreme Court.

Poll rates Gary Cooper box office king.

## 1954

Ted Mack's *Amateur Hour* is first TV show broadcast in color.

Joe DiMaggio weds Marilyn Monroe.

To celebrate turning nineteen, a young singer named Elvis Presley pays $4 to a Memphis recording studio to record "Casual Love" and "I'll Never Stand

in Your Way."

Cigarette smoking is linked to lung cancer.

Bill Haley and the Comets record "Rock Around the Clock."

Supreme Court orders school integration, setting aside the "separate but equal" doctrine.

In the *Hernández v. Texas* decision, the Supreme Court recognizes Hispanics as a separate class of people who are suffering profound discrimination.

Over the next four years, Operation Wetback deports more than 3.8 million Mexican Americans, most without deportation hearings.

Elvis records "That's All Right."

Marilyn Monroe files for divorce from Joe DiMaggio.

Disney airs first episode of *Davy Crockett* TV series.

IBM demonstrates NORC computer.

William Golding's *Lord of the Flies* is published.

J.R.R. Tolkien's *Lord of the Rings* is published.

Ernest Hemingway wins the Nobel Prize for Literature.

Senate censures McCarthy for conduct unbecoming a senator.

## 1955

United States gives $216 million in aid to South Vietnam.

No-iron Dacron, a knit fabric, debuts.

Con Edison announces plans to build the first nuclear power plant.

Bebop jazz great Charlie Parker dies at 34, as a result of years of drug abuse.

Albert Einstein dies at the age of 76.

USSR establishes permanent commission on interplanetary communication.

Presbyterian Church votes to accept women as ministers.

Disneyland opens in Anaheim,

California.

Chuck Berry records "Maybellene."

James Dean dies in a car accident.

Pop Artist Jasper Johns's *Target with Four Faces* is exhibited.

## 1956

In Montgomery, Alabama, Rosa Parks refuses to give up her seat on a bus to a white passenger, and is arrested.

Whites attack Nat King Cole as he sings to a white audience in Birmingham, Alabama.

U.S. Supreme Court rules that segregation on public transportation is unconstitutional.

Mechanics and Farmers Savings Bank in Bridgeport, Connecticut, opens first drive-up window.

Elvis performs on Ed Sullivan's TV show and breaks audience record with 54 million viewers.

Abstract painter Jackson Pollock dies in a car accident.

Atlantic City report ties lung cancer to air pollution.

John F. Kennedy's *Profiles in Courage*, which goes on to win a Pulitzer Prize, is published.

## 1957

General Electric Corporation announces that it has created a manmade material as hard as a diamond.

Track star Bruce Dean quits the University of Pennsylvania team rather than cut his "Elvis" sideburns.

Pat Boone, wearing his white buck shoes, sells 3 million records.

African-American tennis star Althea Gibson wins Wimbledon.

Youth crime explodes. In New York, persons under twenty-one make up 50 percent of those arrested for robbery and 60 percent of those arrested for burglary.

President Eisenhower sends troops to Arkansas when the state defies integration in its schools.

Soviets surprise the world with the launching of *Sputnik*, the world's first manmade satellite.

Dr. Seuss's *The Cat in the Hat* is published.

## 1958

Linus Pauling presents a petition of 9,000 scientists to the United Nations asking to ban nuclear tests.

Elvis is drafted into the army.

U.S. has two thirds of the world's TV sets.

Vanguard satellite reaches orbit. This is America's first successful launch.

American piano virtuoso Van Cliburn, twenty-three years old, wins the Soviet Union's international Tchaikovsky competition.

Arnold Palmer wins Masters golf tournament.

NASA created by bill, allotting millions for U.S. space program.

Pop singer Michael Jackson is born.

Vladimir Nabokov's *Lolita* is published.

Martin Luther King Jr. is arrested for loitering in Alabama and is fined $14.

World's deepest oil well reaches 25,340 feet before being abandoned in Pecos County, Texas.

## 1959

Fidel Castro's forces conquer Cuba.

United States launches first weather station in space, Vanguard II satellite.

Dalai Lama flees Tibet in front of Chinese occupying forces.

Hawaii becomes fiftieth state.

First telephone cable linking United States to Europe is completed.

Scandal erupts over discovery that TV quiz shows have been fixed for years.

Two American soldiers, killed by the Vietcong at Bien Hoa, are the first Americans to die in Vietnam during this era; by the end of the year, there will be 760 U.S. military personnel in Vietnam.

## 1960

Four black students at North Carolina A&T College in Greensboro stage first lunch counter sit-in at local Woolworth's store.

Cuba seizes U.S. assets.

Food and Drug Administration approves first public sale of birth control pills.

New York Circuit Court of Appeals rules that D. H. Lawrence's *Lady Chatterley's Lover* is not obscene.

San Francisco police battle student protesters outside House Un-American Activities Committee hearings.

Student Nonviolent Coordinating Committee (SNCC) is founded.

Nixon-Kennedy debate is watched by largest TV audience ever, 75 million.

John F. Kennedy and Lyndon B. Johnson defeat Richard Nixon and Henry Cabot Lodge in the closest presidential election since 1884.

"Itsy Bitsy Teenie Weenie Yellow Polka Dot Bikini" tops the song charts.

Pepsi begins its "For those who think young" campaign.

During the decade, Mexican-American immigration will increase to 13.9 percent of the total number of immigrants to the United States.

## 1961

United States breaks diplomatic relations with Cuba.

President John F. Kennedy challenges the nation in his inaugural speech to "ask not what your country can do for you; ask what you can do for your country."

President Kennedy creates the Peace Corps with an executive order; 13,000 young Americans apply as volunteers over the next six months.

About 1,500 CIA-trained Cuban rebels make a disastrous attempt to invade Cuba at the Bay of Pigs.

Yuri Gagarin (USSR) becomes first human in space (orbiting for 1 hour, 49 minutes).

Harper Lee's *To Kill a Mockingbird* and Joseph Heller's *Catch-22* are published.

Henry Miller's previously banned *Tropic of Cancer* is published in the United States and reaches the bestseller list.

President Kennedy sends another 100 American military advisers and 400 Special Forces troops to South Vietnam.

President Kennedy urges Americans to set a goal of landing a man on the moon before the end of the decade.

Two busloads of Freedom Riders leave Washington, D.C., for New Orleans to protest segregated bus facilities; in Anniston, Alabama, a bomb hospitalizes twelve passengers.

Alan B. Shepard makes a successful fifteen-minute flight in the Mercury capsule, reaching an altitude of 116.5 miles in a 302-mile suborbital arc; said he had "about 30 seconds to look out the window."

Federal Communications Commission Chairman Newton Minow describes television programming as a "vast wasteland."

The Soviet Union and East Germany begin erecting a wooden and barbed-wire fence along the 25-mile border between East and West Berlin; within three days they will build the Berlin Wall, which will seal off access and become a Cold War symbol.

Advisers recommend that President Kennedy increase military aid and commit 6,000 to 8,000 troops to South Vietnam.

President Kennedy sends his first military personnel, 400 helicopter crewmen, to South Vietnam.

President Kennedy establishes the President's Commission on the Status of Women, headed by Eleanor Roosevelt.

The postwar Baby Boom crests with a record 4.27 million births.

The Supremes sign with Motown and release their first records.

Ray Kroc buys out the McDonald brothers for $14 million and founds the McDonald's chain with 200 restaurants.

Movies *Splendor in the Grass* and *Raisin in the Sun* premiere.

Coca-Cola introduces the no-return glass bottle.

## 1962

President Kennedy announces that American noncombatant troops in Vietnam have been ordered to fire if fired upon.

John H. Glenn Jr. is the first American astronaut to orbit the earth, circling it three times.

Pentagon verifies reports that American pilots are flying combat missions in Vietnam.

Secretary of Defense Robert J. McNamara confirms that American soldiers are exchanging fire with the Vietcong.

*Cosmopolitan* editor Helen Gurley Brown publishes *Sex and the Single Girl*.

Students for a Democratic Society hold national convention at Port Huron, Michigan.

In *Engel v. Vitale* Supreme Court decides, 6-1, that prayer in public schools is unconstitutional.

César Chávez founds United Farm Workers union.

After riots that resulted in two deaths and hundreds of injuries, James Meredith is the first black student to attend the University of Mississippi, under federal guard.

American pilots in Vietnam shoot first despite orders to fire only in defense.

Soviets back down from U.S. blockade of Cuba to end the missile crisis.

Rachel Carson warns of environmental pollution in *Silent Spring*.

*Dr. No*, the first James Bond film, premiers.

After losing the California gubernatorial race, Richard Nixon tells reporters, "You won't have Dick Nixon to kick around anymore."

Dulles Airport opens in Washington, D.C., and is the first airport designed for jets in the United States.

The last of the Bay of Pigs survivors are ransomed from Castro.

Reports confirm 11,000 American advisers and technicians are aiding South Vietnam.

## 1963

United Press International reports that thirty Americans have been killed in Vietnam combat.

Betty Friedan publishes *The Feminine Mystique*, a critique of the cultural, social, and economic limits imposed on middle-class women.

Civil rights groups conduct Mississippi voter-registration drive.

Supreme Court rules that indigents are entitled to free counsel in *Clarence v. Gideon*.

Martin Luther King Jr. is arrested after leading assault against segregation in Alabama, where he writes "Letter from a Birmingham Jail."

Demonstrations against discrimination in schools, employment, and housing are held through the country; nearly 14,000 persons are arrested in seventy-five Southern cities.

Harvard University fires research psychologists Richard Alpert and Timothy Leary for experimenting with LSD.

Buddhist monk dies from self-immolation protesting religious persecution in South Vietnam.

Charles Schultz's *Happiness Is a Warm Puppy* makes the bestseller list.

During his swearing-in ceremony, Alabama Governor George Wallace pledges "segregation now, segregation tomorrow, segregation forever."

Medgar Evers, field secretary for the National Association for the Advancement of Colored People in Mississippi, is murdered entering his home in Jackson; two trials end in hung juries.

Martin Luther King Jr. delivers "I Have a Dream" speech before a crowd of 200,000 to conclude the March on Washington.

In Crystal City, the Political Association of Spanish-Speaking Organizations and local Teamsters unite to take over the city council for two years.

A direct telephone link, called the "Hotline," between Soviet Union and the United States is installed.

Four young girls are killed when the 16th Street Baptist Church is bombed in Birmingham, Alabama; the last bomber was finally convicted in 2002.

With the CIA's knowledge, South Vietnamese President Ngo Dinh Diem and his brother are killed in a coup.

American military personnel in Vietnam number 16,800.

La Alianza Federal de Mercedes (The Federal Land Grant Alliance) is incorporated by Reies López Tijerina.

President Kennedy is assassinated in Dallas, Texas; Lee Harvey Oswald is charged.

Jack Ruby kills Oswald.

Newly sworn-in President Lyndon B. Johnson appoints commission headed by

Chief Justice Earl Warren to investigate Kennedy's assassination.

Hit songs include "Puff (the Magic Dragon)," "Blowin' in the Wind," and "The Times They Are A-Changin'."

## 1964

The U.S. Surgeon General's special committee report, *Smoking and Health*, links cigarette smoking with cancer and calls for federal regulation of cigarettes.

The Twenty-fourth Amendment to the Constitution, forbidding poll or other taxes used to qualify voters in federal elections, takes effect.

President Johnson appoints Lieutenant General William C. Westmoreland to replace General Paul Harkins as head of the United States Military Assistance Command in South Vietnam.

After ending a seventy-five-day filibuster, the Senate passes the Civil Rights Act of 1964 to ban discrimination in education, employment, and public places; President Johnson signs the bill July 2.

Food Stamp program begins.

Three civil rights workers participating in the Student Nonviolent Coordinating Committee's movement to encourage voter registration are arrested for speeding in Mississippi, held for six hours, and are not seen again; their bodies are found buried in a dam on August 4.

The Federal Trade Commission announces that cigarette packages must carry a health warning label beginning in 1965.

The movies *Dr. Strangelove*, *My Fair Lady*, *Mary Poppins*, and *The Pink Panther* premiere.

Lester Maddox, later elected governor of Georgia in January 1967 on a segregationist platform, encourages the use of ax handles against black persons entering his restaurant.

Since December, American casualties in Vietnam have totaled 1,387.

Rioting begins in New York City after a police officer shoots and kills a fifteen-year-old black male during a disturbance, touching off riots in many northern cities; this would be the first of several "long, hot summers."

The United States increases its troop commitment in Vietnam to 21,000.

President Johnson announces on national television that the North Vietnamese have attacked two U.S. destroyers in international waters in the Gulf of Tonkin.

The House of Representatives approves by a vote of 416-0 the Gulf of Tonkin Resolution, approving "all necessary measures by the President to repel any armed attack against U.S. forces"; only two members of the Senate, Wayne Morse (R-OR) and Ernest Gruening (D-AK), oppose the resolution.

A special seven-member commission, headed by Chief Justice Earl Warren, unanimously concludes that Lee Harvey Oswald acted alone when he assassinated President Kennedy.

At age thirty-five, Martin Luther King Jr. is the youngest recipient of the Nobel Peace Prize for the "furtherance of brotherhood among men."

With 43.13 million votes to Republican candidate Barry Goldwater's 27.8 million votes, President Johnson wins the election by the greatest popular vote landslide in American history.

The braless look becomes fashionable.

Beatles tour the United States and are met by 10,000 fans at JFK airport in New York.

The Free Speech Movement of the University of California at Berkeley ends when police arrest 796 student demonstrators.

The FBI arrests twenty-one white men on conspiracy charges related to the deaths of the three civil rights workers; a week later the charges are dismissed on a technicality.

## 1965

In his State of the Union Address, President Johnson promises a "Great Society" that will improve the quality of life for all Americans; his budget is the greatest expansion of domestic welfare programs since Franklin D. Roosevelt's New Deal.

President Johnson orders the first air strike against North Vietnam in response to a Vietcong attack against the U.S. military barracks at Pleiku, which killed thirty-two Americans; two weeks later American planes begin dropping napalm, an incendiary chemical.

Rodolfo "Corky" Gonzáles is appointed director of Denver's War on Poverty Program.

Thirty-nine-year-old black nationalist Malcolm X is shot to death during a rally in Harlem.

In Selma, Alabama, 200 Alabama state troopers using tear gas, whips, and nightsticks stop 525 blacks marching to protest the denial of voting rights; on March 21, after President Johnson mobilizes 4,000 troops, 25,000 people complete the march to Montgomery.

The National Farm Workers Association (César Chávez and Dolores Huerta) meet in a Delano church hall and vote to join the Agricultural Workers Organizing Committee strike.

The Supreme Court unanimously decides that conscientious objector status must be granted for those who believe that registering for the draft is contrary to their religious beliefs.

Chávez's National Farm Workers Association begins the grape boycott, targeting Schenley Industries and DiGiorgio Corp.

The first anti-war "teach-in" takes place at the University of Michigan.

U.S. military personnel in Vietnam increase by 20,000.

Students for Democratic Society organize 15,000 students and others to demonstrate at the White House against American involvement in Vietnam.

President Johnson asks Congress to approve $700 million in addition to the $1.5 billion annual costs already appropriated for the war effort in Vietnam.

Anti-war protests mark Armed Forces Day.

NBC news expands from 15 minutes to 30 minutes; prime-time shows are in color.

The Department of Defense reports that 503 Americans have been killed in Vietnam.

President Johnson announces an increase in military personnel in Vietnam from 75,000 to 125,000, and that he will double the monthly draft quota.

President Johnson signs the long-awaited Medicare bill that provides medical assistance financed through social security for persons over the age of sixty-five.

President Johnson signs the Voting Rights Act of 1965.

During a heat wave, riots break out when police arrest a black drunken driver in the predominantly black Watts area of Los Angeles; six days of violence results in four thousand arrests, $40 million in damage, and thirty-five deaths.

Congress passes a law making it a crime to burn draft cards.

The Department of Housing and Urban Development is established.

Approximately 70,000 to 100,000 pro-testers participate in weekend anti-war protests in forty cities throughout the nation.

20,000 anti-war protesters march in Washington, D.C.

A Quaker, protesting the Vietnam War, burns himself to death in front of the Pentagon.

American troops in Vietnam total 170,000.

The post–World War II Baby Boom, producing over 4 million births a year since 1954, ends as the birthrate falls below 20 per 1,000.

On the final day of a Christmas truce in Vietnam, President Johnson announces that since peace efforts of the past thirty-seven days have failed, the United States will resume bombing raids on North Vietnam.

By the end of this year, American casualties in Vietnam are 1,340 dead, 5,300 wounded, and approximately 150 missing or captured.

First approved by the Food and Drug Administration in 1960 as an oral contraceptive, "the pill" has become a popular adopted phrase.

The Grateful Dead begin performing in San Francisco.

## 1966

Controversy arises over the draft when student demonstrators are reclassified as 1-A, placing them at the top of the draft.

LSD, a hallucinogenic drug, comes under federal regulation.

The first person to be caught burning his draft card is convicted.

The Selective Service announces that college deferments will now be based on academic performance.

About 350 persons buy ad space in the *Washington Post* declaring their refusal to pay taxes to support the Vietnam War.

The U.S. combat toll in Vietnam reaches 3,047.

The United States forces fire on targets in Cambodia for the first time.

President Johnson characterizes those who oppose the war in Vietnam as "nervous Nellies," as 10,000 persons picket the White House and 63,000 have pledged not to vote for any pro–Vietnam War candidate.

Black Power advocate Stokely Carmichael is elected head of the Student Nonviolent Coordinating Committee (SNCC).

The Black Panther Party is formed.

At an EEOC meeting in Albuquerque, only one commissioner shows up, and fifty Chicano leaders, including "Corky" Gonzáles, walk out, protesting the lack of Mexican-American staff and efforts.

*Star Trek* premieres on television, along with *Batman*, *The Smothers Brothers Comedy Hour*, *Mission: Impossible*, *The Monkees*, *The Hollywood Squares*, and *The Dating Game*.

A sniper shoots James Meredith, the first black student to attend the University of Mississippi in 1962, during a "pilgrimage" to Jackson, Mississippi. To show the state's black population it has nothing to fear, the SNCC, Congress of Racial Equality (CORE), and Martin Luther King's Southern Christian Leadership Conference continue the march.

Secretary of Defense Robert McNamara announces that military strength in Vietnam will increase to 285,000.

Rodolfo Acuña starts teaching the first Mexican-American history class in Los Angeles.

César Chávez and the National Farm Workers Association march from Delano to Sacramento.

"Corky" Gonzáles is fired from the

Neighborhood Youth Corps directorship, promising that "this day a new crusade for justice is born." He founds the Crusade for Justice in Denver.

The farm-worker solidarity march from the Rio Grande to Austin takes place.

The first Alianza public protest takes place: a three-day march from Albuquerque to Santa Fe to present demands to the governor.

The AFL-CIO executive council admits the United Farm Workers Organizing Committee, merged from the NFWA and the AWOC.

By a 5–4 margin in its *Miranda v. Arizona* decision, the Supreme Court decides an accused person has the right to remain silent, that an attorney can be present during police interrogation, and that an attorney will be appointed if the defendant cannot afford one.

The House of Representatives' Armed Services Committee recommends lowering the draft age from twenty-two to nineteen or twenty.

Led by Betty Friedan, disillusioned delegates from the President's Commission on the Status of Women form the National Organization for Women (NOW); by fall NOW's membership will reach 300; by the end of the decade, NOW will claim 8,000 members.

Black violence erupts in slum areas in sixteen cities.

After five hours of near-rioting by 4,000 whites, Martin Luther King Jr. says he has "never seen such hate—not in Mississippi or Alabama—as I see in Chicago."

Timothy Leary proclaims LSD as the sacrament of his new religion.

Tijerina and 350 members of La Alianza occupy Kit Carson National

Forest Camp Echo Amphitheater on behalf of Pueblo de San Joaquín de Chama. Within a week, state police, rangers, and sheriff's deputies move in. La Alianza "arrests" two rangers and tries them for trespassing.

The Treasury Department reports that the Vietnam War is costing $4.2 billion a month.

Congress establishes the Department of Transportation.

At 320,000, American troops outnumber regular South Vietnamese troops.

Bestselling books include Jacqueline Susann's *Valley of the Dolls* and Masters and Johnson's *Human Sexual Response*.

A ratings code is instituted by movie studios.

The mental standard of U.S. military inductees is lowered from a score of 16 to 10, out of a possible score of 100.

American fatalities in Vietnam number 6,407.

The United Farm Workers wins a contract with DiGiorgio Corp.

*Time* magazine names "Twenty-five and Under" as its "Man of the Year."

## 1967

Approximately 25,000 hippies pour into Golden Gate Park to conduct the first "be-in."

By the end of the month, 380,000 U.S. troops are in Vietnam.

The Mexican American Youth Organization (MAYO) is formed on college campuses in Texas.

The Twenty-fifth Amendment to the Constitution is ratified, defining presidential succession.

The Alianza Federal de Mercedes changes its name to Alianza Federal de Pueblos Libres.

Sponsored by the Spring Mobilization Committee, the largest anti-war protests to date are held in New York (100,000-

125,000) and San Francisco (75,000).

Riots break out in the black ghetto of Cleveland, the first of 159 riots that will occur this summer.

General Westmoreland criticizes antiwar factions as "unpatriotic."

Mohammed Ali loses his heavyweight boxing title for refusing army induction.

The Mexican-American Legal Defense and Education Fund (MALDEF) is incorporated in San Antonio.

One Jackson State University student dies during rioting.

In New York City, 70,000 demonstrate in support of American military involvement in Vietnam.

The Alianza Federal de Pueblos Libres national convention is held in Albuquerque, organized by Tijerna. Here for the first time the idea for La Raza Unida is discussed.

"Summer of Love" takes place in San Francisco.

Congress gives the president the power to cancel the draft deferments of most graduate students.

Twenty-six are killed during a riot in Newark, New Jersey.

The worst riot of this century breaks out in Detroit, where blacks, who comprise one third of the city's population, are unemployed at double the national average; 2,000 are injured, almost 500 buildings are damaged or destroyed, and 43 people are killed.

Movie premieres include: *The Graduate*, *Guess Who's Coming to Dinner*, *Bonnie and Clyde*, and *In the Heat of the Night*.

President Johnson appoints the Special Advisory Commission on Civil Disorders to investigate the riots in Detroit and 120 other cities.

The United States has 464,000 troops in Vietnam.

President Johnson approves $20 billion for military actions in Vietnam during fiscal year 1968.

In Washington, D.C., an estimated 100,000 people gather at the Lincoln Memorial to protest the war in Vietnam; about 50,000 of the demonstrators then march two miles to the Pentagon to hold a vigil.

250 students representing seven Los Angeles colleges and universities meet to form United Mexican American Students (UMAS).

Tijerina conducts an armed raid in Tierra Amarilla on the Rio Arriba County Courthouse to make a citizen's arrest of D.A. Alfonso Sanchez.

The UFW wins contracts with Gallo, Almaden, Franzia, Paul Mason, Goldberg, the Novitiate of Los Gatos, and Perelli-Minetti.

David Sánchez dissolves Young Citizens for Community Action to form the Brown Berets self-defense group in Los Angeles. The Brown Berets begin a series of pickets in front of sheriff and police stations.

More than 100 Chicanos demonstrate at the East L.A. Sheriff's substation against police brutality.

Following the draft protests, General Lewis B. Hershey, head of the Selective Service System, instructs local draft boards to cancel deferments of persons who have participated in demonstrations.

In response to General Hershey's directive, a coalition of some forty antiwar groups disrupt registration centers nationwide.

The Federal Bureau of Narcotics reports that the number of known drug addicts has increased to almost 60,000, with about half of them between the ages of twenty-one and thirty.

The number of American troops in Vietnam has increased by over 100,000 to a total of 486,000, exceeding the total number of Americans troops involved in the Korean War; the tonnage of bombs dropped in Vietnam exceeds the total tonnage that the United States dropped in Germany during World War II.

The American death toll in Vietnam this year is 9,353, nearly 3,000 more than the previous six years combined.

## 1968

Since January 1, 1961, the total American death toll in Vietnam has risen to 15,997.

Benita Martínez founds *El Grito del Norte* newspaper in Albuquerque.

Vietcong troops launch a surprise massive offensive during the Tet truce in South Vietnam, costing 1,110 American lives.

State police fire at South Carolina State College students attempting to desegregate a local bowling alley; three persons are killed and thirty-seven wounded.

César Chávez begins a twenty-five-day fast at Forty Acres, near Delano. He states he is fasting in penitence for farm workers' moral problems and talk of violence.

Draft deferments are abolished for most graduate students.

The President's National Advisory Commission on Civil Disorders (Kerner Commission) warns that massive black unemployment, unfulfilled civil rights promises, and the government's reluctance to enforce civil rights laws are pushing the country toward two "separate but unequal" societies.

More than 1,000 students peacefully walk out of Abraham Lincoln High School in Los Angeles.

César Chávez breaks his fast at a Mass

in a Delano public park with 4,000 supporters, including Robert Kennedy, at his side.

700 Chicano students walk out of Lanier High School in San Antonio, Texas. Soon 600 more walk out of Edgewood High School.

Denver Chicanos begin a boycott of Coors for discriminatory hiring.

A grand jury indicts the "L.A. 13" for conspiracy to disrupt the peace in organizing the school walkouts.

East L.A. native José Sánchez, nineteen, is the first Chicano to publicly resist the military draft.

Students and parents picket Lincoln High School and the LAUSD Board of Education, demanding teacher Sal Castro's reinstatement.

Chicanos sit-in at the Los Angeles Unified School District Board of Education: thirty-five parents, students, and Brown Berets protest Sal Castro's suspension.

Young Lords Organization (YLO) in Chicago takes over Armitage Street Methodist Church and renames it the People's Church for their headquarters and to start a day care.

LAUSD Board votes to return Sal Castro to the classroom.

UMAS and the Black Student Union (BSU) unite, and Rosalío Muñoz is elected UCLA student body president.

A Gallup poll finds that 49 percent of the respondents feel that committing American troops to Vietnam was a mistake.

Senator Eugene McCarthy of Minnesota wins a surprising 42 percent of the vote in the New Hampshire Democratic primary; President Johnson wins 48 percent.

The number of U.S. combat deaths in Vietnam reaches 19,670.

In a nationally televised speech, President Johnson, with his Gallup poll approval at a record low of 36 percent, announces that he will not seek or accept nomination for another term and that he is unilaterally ordering a halt of the bombing in North Vietnam.

While supporting a strike of black garbage collectors in Memphis, Martin Luther King Jr. is shot to death; forty-six persons are killed in race riots in Washington, D.C., New York City, Chicago, Detroit, and 100 other cities.

President Johnson signs the Civil Rights Act of 1968, also known as the Fair Housing Act, prohibiting racial discrimination in the sale and rental of houses and apartments.

At Columbia University in New York City, 800 to 1,000 students occupy several campus buildings to protest Columbia's ties to Pentagon-funded research and the university's plans to erect a gymnasium in a low-cost housing area.

The United States and North Vietnam open peace talks in Paris.

Nine anti-war protesters, led by the Revs. Philip and Daniel Berrigan, burn 400 draft records at the Selective Service headquarters in Catonsville, Maryland.

Shortly after his win in the California Democratic primary, Robert F. Kennedy is assassinated in Los Angeles.

Protesters at the Miss America Pageant throw bras, girdles, and high heels into a "freedom trash can."

"Consciousness-raising" begins in women's liberation groups.

General Creighton W. Abrams takes over the command of U.S. troops in Vietnam from General Westmoreland.

American troops in Vietnam total 541,000.

New books include Eldridge Cleaver's *Soul on Ice* and Tom Wolfe's *The Electric Kool-Aid Acid Test*.

Richard M. Nixon wins the Republican presidential nomination in Miami Beach; Spiro T. Agnew is his running mate.

The FBI reports 61,843 state marijuana arrests, a 98 percent increase from 1966.

An estimated 30 percent of the population attends elementary and secondary schools; 950 colleges register 1.6 million students, a 50 percent increase since 1963.

President Johnson announces the end of all bombing in North Vietnam, and Hanoi agrees to include the South Vietnamese government and the National Liberation Front, or Vietcong, in the negotiations in Paris.

In one of the closest elections in American history, Richard M. Nixon wins the presidency with 43.4 percent of the popular vote, beating Democratic candidate Hubert Humphrey and American party candidate George Wallace.

Members of the newly formed American Indian Movement (AIM) capture national public attention by occupying Alcatraz Island in San Francisco Bay.

The number of American combat fatalities in Vietnam reaches 30,057 as troop levels increase to 540,000 during the year.

Yale College begins admitting women.

*Hair* premieres off-off-Broadway.

Between June 1963 and May 1968, some 15,000 persons are arrested during 369 major civil rights demonstrations.

1969

After ten weeks of deliberations, American and North Vietnamese delegates agree on the shape of the table to be used when the South Vietnamese and National Liberation Front representatives join the talks.

The American combat death toll in Vietnam—33,641—has surpassed the 33,629 lives lost during the Korean War; by the end of the month, U.S. troops will peak at 543,482.

Governor Ronald Reagan orders the National Guard to spray anti-war protesters with the same skin-stinging powder used against the Vietcong in Vietnam at the University of California at Berkeley campus.

President Nixon announces the withdrawal of 25,000 troops from Vietnam.

A radical splinter group of Students for a Democratic Society called Weathermen carry out violent demonstrations in Chicago.

Chicago YLO takes over a vacant lot that was slated to be a $1,000–membership private tennis club and transforms it into a children's park.

The First National Chicano Youth Liberation Conference is sponsored by the Crusade for Justice.

A three-day conference is organized at Santa Barbara by the Chicano Coordinating Council of Higher Education to create a plan for curricular changes and provide service to Chicano students. Student organizations statewide change their name to El Movimiento Estudiantil Chicano de Aztlán (MEChA).

East Harlem Garbage Offensive in *El Barrio* is organized by Young Lords Party (YLP) in NYC.

The first "Chicano Liberation Day" is organized by "Corky" Gonzáles.

YLP establishes a free breakfast program and testing for lead poisoning and TB, leading to NYC investigations into epidemics.

Rosalío Muñoz burns his draft card at the induction center in downtown Los Angeles.

YLP opens office in Newark.

People's Church Offensive take over Methodist Church at Lexington Avenue and 111th Street after congregation refused to allow Young Lords to run community programs at the church.

Católicos por la Raza clashes with police as it demands church programs for Chicanos in front of St. Basil's Cathedral in Los Angeles.

Several days of rioting and marches follow a police raid on Stonewall Inn, a gay bar in New York City's Greenwich Village.

First conference of La Raza, a Chicano rights political group, is held in Denver.

Astronaut Neil Armstrong is the first person to land on the moon.

H. Rap Brown resumes his leadership of SNCC.

More than 400,000 attend a three-day rock festival at Woodstock in upstate New York.

The *New York Times* reports that the United States is "torn by dissent" over the issue of sex education in public schools.

The First National Moratorium Day observance draws thousands of people to protest the Vietnam War, including many members of the middle class; Coretta Scott King, widow of Dr. Martin Luther King Jr., leads 45,000 in a candlelight parade past the White House.

Vice President Spiro Agnew labels anti-war demonstrators as "an effete corps of impudent snobs who characterize themselves as intellectuals"; a poll shows that 55 percent of Americans responding sympathize with the protesters.

Lieutenant William Calley Jr. is charged with the murders of unarmed South Vietnamese men, women, and children at the village of My Lai.

In the largest anti-war demonstration to date, the National Mobilization Committee to End the War in Vietnam attracts 800,000 mostly white, middle-class people to protest in Washington, D.C.

*Sesame Street* premieres.

Movies include: *I am Curious (Yellow)*, *Bob and Carol and Ted and Alice*, and *Easy Rider*.

*Oh! Calcutta*, the first nude musical, opens.

The Selective Service System conducts the first draft lottery since 1942.

President Nixon announces the third American troop withdrawal from South Vietnam, bringing the total withdrawal to 115,000.

## 1970

The first Earth Day (April 22) symbolizes the emerging environmental movement; an estimated 30 million Americans protest the pollution of the environment in the largest demonstration in history.

An American offensive into Cambodia triggers a wave of protests around the country; at Kent State University in Ohio, National Guardsmen kill four students and wound nine others in 15 seconds of gunfire.

Between 60,000 and 100,000 demonstrators peacefully gather in Washington, D.C., to protest the Cambodian incursion.

A noontime rally in New York City draws an estimated 60,000 to 150,000 construction workers, longshoremen, and others who support White House policy in Vietnam.

Police fire into a crowd of students at Jackson State College in Mississippi, killing two students and wounding twelve; a federal grand jury fails to return any indictments.

The Environmental Protection Agency is created by Congress.

The United States Commission on Campus Unrest reports that a crisis on American college campuses could threaten "the very survival of the nation."

Hit songs include "Do the Funky Chicken" and "We've Only Just Begun."

The Beatles disband.

Chicago YLO opens a free health clinic in the basement of the People's Church.

YLP opens office in the Bronx.

YLP begins publishing a newspaper, *Palante*, and broadcasting a weekly radio program on WBAI.

The Second National Chicano Moratorium Committee demonstration takes place in L.A. with 6,000 people.

La Raza Unida Party wins four of seven seats on the Crystal City school board.

YLP seizes NYC TB testing van.

The first Colorado La Raza Unida meeting takes place at Southern Colorado State College. "Corky" Gonzáles is elected state chair.

In the Lincoln Hospital Offensive, YLP demands better services for South Bronx residents by taking over vacant building in hospital complex to run TB and lead poisoning detection programs and create a day care.

The National Chicano Moratorium Committee marches in Houston, drawing 5,000 people.

YLP opens offices on Lower East Side of Manhattan and in Philadelphia.

The third Moratorium protest in Laguna Park, with 10,000–30,000 people attending. A liquor store theft provides police with an excuse to break up the peaceable gathering. Some protesters respond by throwing things back. At the Silver Dollar Bar, Rubén Salazar is shot in the head with a tear gas missile.

More than 600 Chicano students walk out of an East Chicago, Indiana, school after the vice principal says "Mexicans are lazy and ignorant."

L.A. County District Attorney Evelle J. Younger announces he will not prosecute Deputy Thomas Wilson for Salazar's death.

Funeral march for Julio Roldán protesting this Young Lord's suspicious prison death.

Second takeover of the People's Church occurs.

March to United Nations of 10,000 people recognizing the anniversary of the Puerto Rican Nationalist Party.

The Oakland-Berkeley chapter of La Raza Unida Party has its first meeting.

*Everything You Ever Wanted to Know About Sex but Were Afraid to Ask* makes the best-seller list.

Approximately 9,200 drug violations are recorded among American soldiers in Vietnam.

Since January 1, 1961, 44,241 Americans have been killed in Vietnam.

## 1971

Cigarette advertising is banned from television.

The number of American troops in Vietnam drops to 184,000.

Anti-war demonstrations climax in Washington, D.C., as thousands try to close down the government by disrupting city traffic.

Peace negotiations over Vietnam begin their fourth year.

The FBI Counter Intelligence Program infiltrates and provokes Chicano organizations.

The Houston Chicana Conference attracts more than 600 Chicanas from twenty-three states.

La Marcha de la Reconquista, a march from Calexico to Sacramento, begins

with Rosalío Muñoz, David Sánchez, and the Brown Berets.

The Twenty-sixth Amendment to the Constitution, giving eighteen-year-olds the right to vote, is ratified in a record two months and seven days.

The Supreme Court, by a 6–1 margin, upholds the right of the *New York Times* and the *Washington Post* to publish the "Pentagon Papers."

## 1972

The National Commission on Marijuana and Drug Abuse reveals that 24 million Americans—40 percent of the eighteen- to twenty-five-year-old group—have smoked marijuana at least once.

A security guard finds burglars in the Democratic party headquarters at the Watergate Hotel complex.

In its 5–4 *Furman v. Georgia* decision, the Supreme Court declares the death penalty unconstitutional.

Ramsey Muñoz announces his bid for Texas governor under La Raza Unida Party banner at a press conference in San Antonio.

The United Farm Workers Organizing Committee (UFWOC) charters the UFW, AFL-CIO.

The UFW files suit in Phoenix to bar enforcement of the new Arizona Agricultural Relations Act, which will prohibit harvest-time picketing.

The Brown Berets invade Catalina Island and take a campsite in late August, early September.

La Raza Unida Party holds its national convention in El Paso. Some 3,000 Chicanos attend. Gutiérrez beats Gonzales for the national chair in a divisive campaign that leads to the division of the LRUP into two camps.

Muñoz garners 6.2 percent of the gubernatorial vote, nearly undermining

Democrat Dolph Brisco's victory.

AIM occupies a Bureau of Indian Affairs office in Washington, D.C.

Equal Rights Amendment passes House and Senate, goes to states for ratification

Phyllis Schlaffly forms "Stop ERA."

Actress Jane Fonda makes an anti-war speech in North Vietnam, earning her the nickname "Hanoi Jane."

*Ms.* magazine begins publication.

*Life* magazine ends publication after 36 years.

President Nixon wins re-election, capturing forty-nine states.

## 1973

Anti-war demonstrations dampen President Nixon's inauguration.

Worldwide energy crisis spurs economic recession in the United States.

By a 7–2 margin, the Supreme Court legalizes unrestricted abortion during the first trimester of pregnancy in *Roe v. Wade*.

AIM members occupy Wounded Knee, South Dakota.

President Nixon announces that Henry Kissinger and North Vietnamese foreign minister Le Duc Tho have agreed in Paris "to end the war and bring peace with honor in Vietnam and Southeast Asia."

After fourteen years of war in Vietnam, American combat deaths number 46,226, and 10,326 noncombatant deaths.

The seven-member Select Committee on Presidential Campaign Activities opens televised hearings on the origin and activities related to the Watergate break-in.

An advocate of law and order, Vice President Spiro Agnew resigns from office after pleading nolo contendere to charges of income tax evasion.

Representative Gerald R. Ford is

sworn in as the new vice president.

A shootout with police takes place at a Chicano Crusade apartment building, Escuela Tlatelolco, next door to its headquarters.

More than 800 gay organizations have been formed to offer support and education for gay men and women.

**1974**

The Supreme Court rules, 9–0, that President Nixon cannot invoke executive privilege to block the release of sixty-four Watergate-related tapes to the U.S. District Court Judge John Sirica.

Nixon is the first president to resign from office.

Gerald R. Ford is sworn in as the thirty-eighth president.

The Southwest Voter Registration Education Project is established. Willie Valásquez, a former member of MAYO and La Raza Unida, becomes its director.

Raúl Castro becomes the fist Chicano governor of Arizona.

Little League baseball is opened to girls.

**1975**

An American airlift delivers 1,400 Amerasian orphans to the United States.

Congress denies President Ford's request for nearly $1 billion in military and humanitarian aid for South Vietnam.

When the North Vietnamese launch a massive rocket attack on the Saigon airport, President Ford orders the remaining 1,000 Americans and 5,500 South Vietnamese evacuated to offshore ships.

South Vietnam surrenders to the North Vietnamese.

The Indian Self-Determination and Educational Assistance Act is made law, guaranteeing American Indians far more power and additional federal funds to govern their own reservations and to control their children's education.

Voting Rights Act of 1965 is extended to Hispanic Americans.

## SELECTED BIBLIOGRAPHY

Abramson, Michael, and Young Lords Party. *Palante: Young Lords Party.* Photographs by Michael Abramson. McGraw-Hill, NY, 1971.

Albert, Judith Clavir, and Stewart Edward Albert, eds. *The Sixties Papers: Documents of a Rebellious Decade.* Praeger, 1984.

Anderson, Terry H. *The Movement and the Sixties.* Oxford University Press, 1995.

Anderson, Terry H. *The Sixties.* 2nd ed. Pearson/Longman, 2004.

Arturo, Rosales F. *Chicano: The History of the Mexican American Civil Rights Movement.* Arte Publico, 1996.

Carson, Clayborne. *In Struggle: SNCC and the Black Awakening of the 1960s.* Harvard University Press, 1981.

Dickstein, Morris. *Gates of Eden: American Culture in the Sixties.* Basic Books, 1977.

Echols, Alice. *Daring to Be Bad: Radical Feminism in America, 1967–1975.* University of Minnesota Press, 1989.

Evans, Sara. *Personal Politics: The Roots of Women's Liberation in the Movement and the New Left.* Random House, 1979.

Farber, David. *The Age of Great Dreams: America in the 1960s.* Hill and Wang, 1994.

Farber, David, ed. *The Sixties: From Memory to History.* University of North Carolina Press, 1994.

Gitlin, Todd. *The Sixties: Years of Hope, Days of Rage.* Bantam Books, 1987.

Gitlin, Todd. *The Whole World Is Watching: Mass Media in the Making and Unmaking of the New Left.* University of California Press, 1980.

Halberstam, David. *The Fifties.* Fawcett, 1983.

Hampton, Henry, and Steve Fayer. *Voices of Freedom: An Oral History of the Civil Rights Movement from the 1950s through the 1980s.* Bantam Books, 1990.

Jones, Landon Y. *Great Expectations: America and the Baby Boom Generation.*
Coward-McCann, 1980.

King, Mary. *Freedom Song: A Personal Story of the 1960s Civil Rights Movement.* Morrow, 1987.

Kurlansky, Mark. *1968: The Year that Rocked the World.* Ballantine, 2004.

Miller, Jim. *Democracy Is in the Streets: From Port Huron to the Siege of Chicago.* Simon & Schuster, 1970.

Noriega, Chon A., ed. *¿Just Another Poster? Chicano Graphic Arts in California.* Santa Barbara, 2001.

Perrett, Geoffrey. *A Dream of Greatness: The American People 1945–1963.* Coward, McCann & Geoghegan, 1979.

Perry, Charles. *The Haight-Ashbury: A History.* Wenner Books, 2005.

Powers, Thomas. *The War at Home: Vietnam and the American People, 1964–1968.* Grossman Publishers, 1973.

Sale, Kirkpatrick. *SDS.* Random House, 1973.

Schell, Jonathan. *The Time of Illusion.* Knopf, 1976.

Unger, Irwin, and Debi Unger. *The Times Were a Changin': A Sixties Reader.* Three Rivers Press, 1998.

Van Deburg, William L. *New Day in Babylon: The Black Power Movement and American Culture, 1965–1975.* University of Chicago Press, 1992.

Viorst, Milton. *Fire in the Streets: America in the 1960s.* Simon & Schuster, 1979.

Wells, Tom. *The War Within: America's Battle over Vietnam.* University of California Press, 1994.

Wittstock, Laura W., and Elaine J. Salinas. *A Brief History of the American Indian Movement.* American Indian Movement (AIM).

Zaroulis, Nancy, and Gerald Sullivan. *Who Spoke Up? American Protest against the War in Vietnam, 1963–1975.* Doubleday, 1984.

## WEB SITES

Black Arts Movement, http://www.english.uiuc.edu/maps/black arts/blackarts.htm

The Black Panthers, http://www.blackpanther.org/

The Free Speech Movement Archives, http://www.fsm-a.org/

The History of CORE (Congress of Racial Equality). Congress of Racial Equality, http://www.core-online.org/ history/history%20opening.htm

The History of the National Organization for Women. National Organization for Women. http://www.now.org/history/history.html

Jackson, Rebecca. *The 1960s: A Bibliography.* http://www.public.iastate. edu/~rjackson/webbibl.html

Laughead, George. *History: USA: 1960–1969.* WWW Virtual Library. http://vlib.iue.it/history/USA/ERAS/20 TH/1960s.html

Noble, Eric. *The Digger Archives.* http://www.diggers.org/

Pawluk, Adam, Scott Griffin, Mark Andrews, and Mark Monaco. *SNCC, 1960–1966: Six Years of the Student Non-Violent Coordinating Committee.* ibiblio.org. http://www.ibiblio.org/sncc/

*The Sixties: 1954–1974. A Biography of America.* Annenberg/CPB. http://www.learner.org/biography ofamerica/prog24/index.html

Tal, Kalí, ed. *The Sixties Project.* Institute for Advanced Technology in the Humanities (IATH), University of Virginia. http://lists.village.virginia.edu/ sixties/HTML_docs/Sixties.html

Westbrook, Robert, ed. *America in the Sixties: Culture and Counter-Culture.* Yale–New Haven Teachers Institute, 1983, vol. 4. http://www.yale.edu/ynhti/ curriculum/guides/1983/4/

*Grateful acknowledgement is made to the following for permission to reprint previously published material.*

Page 26, By Damien Cave, Matt Diehl, Gavin Edwards, Jenny Eliscu, et al. From *Rolling Stone*, June 24, 2004 © Rolling Stone LLC 2004.

Page 55, Copyright © 1963 by Warner Bros. Inc. Copyright renewed 1991 by Special Rider Music. All rights reserved. International copyright secured. Reprinted by permission.

Page 57, Words and music by Joe McDonald © 1965. Copyright renewed 1993 by Alkatraz Corner Music Co. BMI.

Page 59, From *Gary Snyder Reader* by Gary Snyder. Reprinted by permission of Counterpoint Press, a member of the Perseus Group.

Pages 88 and 89, From *The Leroi Jones/Amiri Baraka Reader* by Imamu Amiri Baraka. Copyright © 2000. Reprinted by permission of the publisher, Thunder Mouth Press, A Division of the Avalon Publishing Group, Inc.

Pages 93–95, From *The Feminine Mystique* by Betty Friedan. Copyright © 1983, 1974, 1973, 1963 by Betty Friedan. Used by permission of W. W. Norton & Company, Inc.

Pages 117–119, "I Am Joaquín" is reprinted with permission from the publisher of *Message to Aztlán* by Rodolfo "Corky" Gonzáles (Houston: Arte Público Press—University of Houston, 2001).

## ILLUSTRATION CREDITS

Pages ii, 3, 5, 8, 9, 12, 19, 22, 29, 33, 34, 35, 36, 37, 40, 41, 43, 44 top and bottom, 46–47, 49, 50, 53, 57 bottom. 60 bottom right, 61 top right, 69, 79, 80, 81, 83, 85, 88, 89, 95, 99, 100, 102, 103, 113, 121 top and bottom, 139, Courtesy of the Library of Congress.

Pages x, 1, 2, 5 center, 7, 10, 13, 21 bottom, 23, 52, 58 and 59, 70, 144, Courtesy of author's collection.

Page 4, Courtesy of State Museum of PA, PA Historical and Museum Commission.

Page 6, Courtesy of Bayer Healthcare LLC.

Page 11, "cover" by James Avati, from *The Catcher in the Rye* by J. D. Salinger, copyright © 1951 by NAL. Used by permission of Dutton Signet, a division of Penguin Group (USA) Inc.

Page 16, Courtesy of Hirshhorn Museum and Sculpture Garden, Smithsonian Institution, Gift of Joseph H. Hirshhorn, 1972. Photograph of painting by Lee Stalsworth.

Pages 17, 30, 54, Courtesy of Corbis.

Page 21 top, Courtesy of Anna Grady.

Pages 24, 25, 131, Courtesy of NASA

Page 57 top, Courtesy of Bentley Historical Library, University of Michigan.

Pages 60 top left, 135, Courtesy of National Archives

Page 61 bottom right, Courtesy of Corbis

Page 65, Courtesy of Kent State University Libraries and Media Services, Department of Special Collections and Archives.

Pages 62, 97, Courtesy of AP/Wide World Photos.

Pages 72–73, Courtesy of R. Crumb.

Pages 74, 137, 140, 141, Courtesy of Robert Altman.

Page 88, Courtesy of The Bancroft Library, University of California, Berkeley.

Page 101, by permission of *Our Bodies, Ourselves*.

Page 106, Courtesy of Ilka Hartmann.

Page 110, Courtesy of Michelle Vignes.

Pages 114–115, 116, 119, Courtesy of Denver Public Library.

Page 122, Courtesy of Oscar Castillo.

Page 125, Courtesy of Los Angeles Times Photographic Archive (Collection 1429). Department of Special Collections, Charles E. Young Research Library, UCLA.

Page 126, Courtesy of the artist Salvador Torres and California Ethnic and Multicultural Archives, UCSB.

Page 129, Courtesy of Michael Abramson.

Page 132, Courtesy of Yale Collection of American Literature, Beinecke Rare Book and Manuscript Library.

Page 134, Courtesy of Cleveland State University Library.

Page 146, Courtesy of Fred W. McDarrah.

# AMERICA
# DREAMING